Woman of God?
Break The Pattern. Keep The Promise

by Big Brother Jeff

SMR Solutions
www.BigBrotherJeff.com
443-308-8063 | info@smrsolutions.org

Copyright © 2026 SMR Solutions

All rights reserved.

No part of this book may be reproduced, distributed, or transmitted in any form or by any means, including photocopying, recording, or other electronic or mechanical methods, without the prior written permission of the publisher, except in the case of brief quotations embodied in critical reviews and certain other noncommercial uses permitted by copyright law.

Title: Woman Of God?
Subtitle: Break The Pattern Keep The Promise
Author: Big Brother Jeff
Publisher: SMR Solutions
Website: www.BigBrotherJeff.com

ISBN: 979-8-218-92890-2 (Paperback)

Printed in the United States of America

Letter to the Reader

Little sisters, This is your big brother Jeff, writing to you from sanctuary. I have been watching the way you move online. The captions. The prayers. The "God send my husband" posts. The hunger is real and the desire is not the problem. Wanting love, safety, stability, and a home is not evil, it is what God wants too. Wanting a closer walk with God is not corny, it is calling. And I need you to hear this clearly before you read one page of this book.

This is not a condemnation letter.

The Father made you with weight. With gifts. With spiritual force. There is something about the faith of a woman that shifts atmospheres. When a woman believes in God, rooms change. Families change. Men straighten up. Children breathe easier. Somewhere along the journey, though, sisters, a lot of you got pulled off track. Not because you are stupid. Not because you are bad.

Not because you are "too far gone."

But simply because the enemy, the devil, is a very patient liar. He does not destroy you quickly or in an obvious way. He grooms you slowly. He reconfigured your perception with influence over time. He trains you to perceive bondage as "self love" and call rebellion "strength." He whispers that your value is your appearance. That your degree is your identity.

And then he does the slickest part.

He convinces you that you are still walking with God at the same time... while in reality you are walking in the opposite direction. So you start speaking spiritual language, but living in patterns that block blessing. You start praying for promise, but practicing traits God warns against. You start asking for "all these things" without seeking God first.

Jesus already told us the order:

> "Seek ye first the kingdom of God, and his righteousness;
> and all these things shall be added unto you."
>
> *Matthew 6:33*

Not seek money first, Not seek attention first. Not seek image first. Because righteousness is not a vibe. It is alignment. You know you are walking with God when your behavior starts looking like His behavior. And you do not discover His behavior by guessing. You discover it by reading His word and being honest about what it praises and what it condemns. You look at who God approved, and why. You look at who God opposed, and why. Then you pull the traits out like fingerprints.

That is what this book is.

A mirror.

A checklist.

A map back home.

Little sister, come back to your foundation.

Come back to the Word.

Come back to dominion.

With love, Big Brother Jeff

How to Use This Book

Most people do not struggle because they lack desire or sincerity. They struggle because their understanding is incomplete. Many behaviors are misnamed. Some traits are minimized. Others are rationalized, spiritualized, or mistaken for something harmless. What often goes unnoticed is that a pattern does not have to feel extreme to be unrighteous. It only has to be misaligned. It is entirely possible to be wrestling with destructive traits while believing they are normal, justified, or even virtuous. It is also possible to be fighting the wrong enemy because the true one has never been correctly identified.

This book was written to correct that problem.

Each chapter isolates a specific trait and examines it plainly, without euphemism or exaggeration. The goal is precision. Once a trait is properly defined, it becomes recognizable. Once it is recognizable, it becomes addressable. And once it is addressed, it can be removed. Transformation does not begin with effort. It begins with accurate diagnosis. This book is meant to be read deliberately. One chapter at a time. Not as a source of affirmation, but as a tool for clarity. The value of what is written here is not in how it makes you feel, but in how clearly it allows you to see.

You cannot confront what you cannot name.

You cannot correct what you do not understand.

You cannot defeat an enemy you never see coming.

Use this book accordingly.

Table of Contents

Chapter 1: Control 8

Chapter 2: Manipulation 15

Chapter 3: Deception and Image Management 22

Chapter 4: Sexual Immorality and Sexual Leverage 29

Chapter 5: Contempt 36

Chapter 6: Pride 43

Chapter 7: Dishonor and Rejection of Headship 50

Chapter 8: Quarrelsome and Contentious 58

Chapter 9: Greed, Materialism, and Serving Mammon 65

Chapter 10: Jealousy and Envy 72

Chapter 11: Rebellion 79

Chapter 12: Witchcraft, Sorcery, and Spiritual Syncretism 86

Chapter 13: Vindictiveness 94

Chapter 14: Disobedience and Stubbornness 102

Chapter 15: Weak Discernment (Easily Fooled) 108

Chapter 16: Disloyalty and Opportunism 114

Chapter 17: Selfishness and Self Centeredness 121

Chapter 18: Gossip, Slander, and Loose Speech 128

Chapter 19: Immodesty and Lack of Discretion 134

Chapter 20: Harshness 141

Chapter 21: Doubtful or Lacking Faith 147

Chapter 22: Idolatry 153

Chapter 23: Unfaithful 160

Chapter 1

Control

Core Lie

"If I do not manage this, everything will fall apart."
"If I am not steering, I am not safe."
"If I do not stay on top of people, outcomes, and timing, I will be punished by uncertainty."

Control is not just preference. It is an inner government. It is the decision that says: I do not trust God to carry outcomes, so I will carry them myself. And because you cannot actually carry outcomes, control always turns into pressure.

◆

How This Shows Up in Real Life

Control is rarely announced. It is usually justified. You call it leadership, but it is domination. You call it standards, but it is fear. You call it discernment, but it is suspicion that will not rest. It shows up like this:

Communication control

You do not just speak, you steer. You ask questions that are not questions. They are traps designed to force a specific answer. You send follow up messages to manage tone. You rewrite conversations in real time so the other person cannot land anywhere except where you want. You do not allow silence to exist. Silence makes you feel powerless, so you fill it with pressure.

Emotional control

You escalate when you feel the outcome slipping. Your tone changes. Your face changes. Your energy shifts. Everyone can feel the room tighten. You punish with withdrawal, coldness, or distance, not to heal, but to regulate the other person. You do not say, "I need space." You make them pay until they submit.

Decision control

You need the final say, even if you pretend you do not. If a decision is made without you, you treat it like betrayal. You reopen settled decisions because you feel unsettled. You keep circling until the other person is exhausted, then you call it "resolution."

Social control

You manage who gets access to your partner. You isolate through "concerns" and "boundaries" that are really fear of influence you cannot control. You leak private information to shape the narrative. You recruit outsiders to pressure outcomes while pretending you are staying out of it.

Spiritual control

You use God language to make your plan sound holy. You say "God showed me" when you really mean "I decided." You treat disagreement as rebellion, even when your motives are exposed. You do not want alignment. You want compliance. Control is not always loud. Sometimes it is quiet, polite, and socially respectable. But the fruit is the same. People feel managed, not loved.

◆

Biblical Pattern

Scripture repeatedly shows the same control pattern: A woman sees an obstacle. She refuses to accept limits. She uses power, pressure, or plotting to remove what stands in her way. Then the home, the covenant, or the community pays. You see it in Jezebel. She does not persuade. She engineers. She writes letters, recruits false witnesses, and forces outcomes through destruction. 1 Kings 21. You see it in Athaliah. She does not wait for legitimacy. She destroys what threatens her throne. 2 Kings 11:1. You see it in Noadiah and those who tried to make Nehemiah afraid so the work would stop. The strategy is fear, because fear makes people controllable. Nehemiah 6:14. Control is consistently shown as fear driven rule, not righteous leadership. It does not preserve life. It consumes it. The pattern is simple: When fear becomes your inner ruler, you will treat people like levers.

◆

False Version vs Godly Version

False version: "I am just being responsible." Responsible women plan. Responsible women communicate. Responsible women take initiative. But control is different. Control cannot tolerate the risk of another person's freedom. Responsibility says, "Here is what I think and here is why." Control says, "If you do not do this my way, you will pay." Responsibility can release an outcome to God. Control cannot. Control must secure. Godly version: "I will obey and let God govern outcomes." Godly order is not chaos. It is not passivity. It is not pretending you do not care. It is a shift in government. It is moving from self rule to submission.

◆

Mirror Questions

- Answer these without performing.
- Do I need control to feel calm?
- Do I punish people with tone, silence, or withdrawal when I feel powerless?
- Do I keep conversations going until the other person yields?
- Do I use fear, pressure, or urgency to force decisions?
- Do I isolate my partner from voices that could challenge my influence?
- Do I leak private information to shape outcomes?
- Do I treat disagreement like betrayal?
- Do I disguise control as "discernment" or "standards"?
- Do I feel anxious when I cannot predict what someone will do next?
- Do I obey God quickly, or only when I can control the risk?

◆

Trajectory If Untreated

Control does not stay contained. It spreads.

In marriage

Your home becomes tense. Not because there is constant yelling, but because everything has to be managed. A man either becomes passive to survive, or he becomes harsh to resist. Either way, trust dies. Intimacy turns into negotiation. Affection becomes strategic. Peace becomes conditional.

In motherhood

Children learn to hide instead of grow. They learn to avoid instead of confess. They learn that love is linked to performance and compliance.

In faith

You can become religious while still ruling. You will quote Scripture, but not submit to it. You will pray, but still panic. You will worship, but still manage. Control creates the illusion of safety while quietly producing slavery.

◆

Counter Trait: Trust in God and Surrendered Obedience

Core Truth

If God gave the instruction, God is responsible for the outcome. Trust is not a personality trait. It is a government shift. A trusting woman still thinks. She still plans. She still speaks clearly. But she stops trying to rule people in order to feel safe. Trust means you obey God without demanding guarantees. You release timing. You release how people respond. You release the need to secure your image. This is not weakness. This is submission.

Luke 1:38

◆

How Trust Shows Up in Real Life

Trust shows up when you can do the right thing without controlling how it lands. You speak once and stop circling. You make a request without attaching pressure. You allow someone to be uncomfortable without rescuing them or punishing them. You stop policing tone and timing as a way to regulate your anxiety. You let silence exist. You let people process. You let God work without you hovering. Trust shows up when your obedience is private. No witnesses. No validation. No applause. Just alignment.

◆

Replacement Practices

These are not suggestions. They are training.

1. Stop using urgency as a weapon
   If something is truly urgent, it will survive calm speech. Make your request once, clearly, and then stop escalating.
2. Practice "one pass" communication
   Say what you mean once. If the person heard you and disagreed, do not repeat yourself to wear them down. If the person did not understand, clarify once, then stop.
3. Fast from punishment tactics
   No cold silence designed to hurt. No withdrawal designed to scare. No tone shifts designed to control. If you need space, say it plainly. Then take it without theatrics.
4. Restore freedom where you have restricted it
   Open doors you have quietly closed. Stop isolating. Stop monitoring. Stop restricting access through fear.

If you are married, stop treating community as a threat. If you are dating, stop treating accountability as interference.

5. Daily obedience practice
   Pick one clear command from Scripture and obey it the same day. Not when it feels safe. Not when you feel calm. Same day. Control trains delay. Trust trains prompt obedience.

6. Replace outcome obsession with prayer and waiting
   Pray, then wait without panic behavior. No follow up texts to manage tone. No extra conversations to secure agreement. No secondary pressure campaigns through other people. If you cannot wait, you are not trusting. You are managing.

◆

Closing Mirror

Control says: I must carry this. Trust says: God carries what belongs to God. If you keep trying to rule outcomes, you will keep sacrificing peace to maintain the illusion of safety. If you surrender government, you will finally have energy to steward what is actually yours to steward. The question is not whether control "works." It always works short term. That is why it is addictive. The question is what it produces over time.

Chapter 2

Manipulation

Core Lie

> "If I am honest, I might not get what I want."
> "If I ask directly, I might be told no."
> "So I will use pressure, emotion, charm, timing, and indirect tactics to secure the outcome while keeping my hands clean."

Manipulation is control that hides. It is steering without ownership. It is getting your way while pretending you did not ask for it.

◆

How This Shows Up in Real Life

Manipulation does not always look evil. Sometimes it looks emotional. Sometimes it looks spiritual. Sometimes it looks "feminine." The fruit is still the same: someone feels pushed, cornered, or managed.

Emotional leverage

You cry, withdraw, go cold, or go quiet, not because you need space, but because you want them to cave. You escalate emotion when you are not getting agreement. You repeat the point until they give up. You keep the room tense until the other person buys peace by surrendering.

Scripted conversations

You rehearse the dialogue in your head, then walk them into it. You do not bring truth. You bring setup. You ask questions that only have one acceptable answer. If they respond outside your script, you punish them with mood, tone, or withdrawal.

Spiritual cover

You use God language to sanctify what you already decided. "God told me" becomes a shield that blocks questions.

Correction becomes "judgment."

Boundaries become "control."

Disagreement becomes "lack of faith."

This is not spiritual leadership. It is spiritual camouflage.

Triangulation

You do not address the person involved. You recruit pressure. You tell friends, family, or church people the story in a way that forces them to take your side. You call it "seeking counsel" when you are really building an army. You leak private details to control how the situation is seen.

Seduction as steering

You use affection, attention, or sexuality to gain power. You give intimacy to calm conflict without telling truth. You withdraw intimacy to punish and pressure. You use flirtation and desirability as currency. This is not love. It is leverage.

◆

Biblical Pattern

Scripture does not treat manipulation as clever. It treats it as snares. Potiphar's wife pressures Joseph day after day, then frames him when he refuses. Genesis 39:10 to 14. That is manipulation plus false witness plus punishment. Samson's wife presses him with tears until he gives his secret, then she betrays him to her people. Judges 14:15 to 20. Delilah takes money, wears him down, then delivers him. Judges 16:4 to 20. Same pattern. Pressure. Wearing down. Outcome secured. Betrayal hidden until it is too late. Jezebel takes Ahab's seal, writes letters, sets up false witnesses, and engineers Naboth's death. 1 Kings 21:7 to 9. That is manipulation with a crown on it. Power from the shadows. The seductress in Proverbs uses touch, spiritual talk, luxury, and much speech to bend a man. Proverbs 7:13 to 21. It is calculated. Not spontaneous. Manipulation always shares the same heart posture: I do not trust truth to be enough, so I will manufacture an outcome.

◆

False Version vs Godly Version

False version: "I am just emotional"

Emotion is not sin. But using emotion to force compliance is. False emotion performs. False emotion escalates until someone yields. False emotion makes the other person responsible for regulating your inner world. Godly version: Honest communication and emotional integrity Emotional integrity says: my feelings are mine to steward, not tools to control you. Honest communication says what is true without attaching pressure. It does not trap. It does not punish. It does not recruit allies to win. It is clean.

Mirror Questions

- Do I use tears, silence, or coldness to force decisions?
- Do I keep conversations going until the other person gives up?
- Do I rehearse conversations so the other person has no real choice?
- Do I "seek counsel" in a way that turns others against the person involved?
- Do I drop hints instead of speaking plainly?
- Do I use affection or intimacy to steer outcomes?
- Do I escalate emotion when I am not getting agreement?
- Do people feel freer after talking to me, or more tangled?
- Do I hide my real desire behind spiritual language?
- Do I feel entitled to a yes because I feel strongly?

◆

Trajectory If Untreated

Manipulation always grows because it works short term.

In marriage

Trust collapses because nothing feels clean. Your partner stops believing your emotion, even when it is real, because it has been used as leverage. He either caves to keep peace or he hardens to survive. Either way, intimacy becomes unstable. Love becomes negotiation.

In friendships

People start limiting access to you. They stop telling you things because they feel you will use information as a tool.

In faith

Manipulation becomes a counterfeit "discernment" identity. You start believing your tactics are wisdom, and correction feels like persecution. The result is isolation and spiritual drift dressed as strength.

◆

Counter Trait: Honest Communication and Emotional Integrity

Core Truth

My feelings are real, but they are not authority. Truth is authority. God is authority. Emotional integrity is when you can name what you feel and still govern yourself. The lie this replaces is simple: If I feel this strongly, the other person should change. Integrity answers: My feelings are mine to steward, not a weapon to make you comply.

◆

How This Shows Up in Real Life

You speak plainly.

"I felt hurt by that."

Not, "If you loved me you would not do that."

"I need time to calm down."

Not silence designed to punish.

"I disagree, and here is why."

Not hint dropping, sarcasm, or side conversations. You accept no without retaliation. You do not repeat the point to wear them down. You do not raise intensity to gain advantage. You stop recruiting pressure. You address the person involved, directly, privately, and cleanly.

◆

Biblical Pattern

Hannah was in deep distress, and she wept. But she did not weaponize her pain. "Hannah was in bitterness of soul, and prayed unto the Lord, and wept sore." 1 Samuel 1:10. She brought it to God. Upward. Not outward as leverage. She accepted misunderstanding from Eli without punishing him. She did not demand relief from her husband through pressure. Her pain was real, but it did not become a steering tool. That is emotional integrity.

◆

Replacement Practices

1. Practice direct requests
   Say what you want plainly. One sentence. No hints. Example: "I want to talk about what happened tonight." Not: "It's fine" followed by coldness.
2. Remove punishment from your communication
   No silent treatment. No cold withdrawal designed to scare. No mood shifts designed to train the other person. If you need space, say it, then take it cleanly.
3. One pass rule
   State the concern once. If they understood and disagree, stop repeating to win. If they did not

understand, clarify once, then stop. This breaks the wearing down cycle.

4. Confess tactics when you catch them
   When you notice yourself hinting, performing, escalating, or recruiting, stop and name it. "I realize I am trying to steer this with emotion. Let me reset and just say it plainly." That one sentence will kill manipulation faster than any dramatic apology later.

5. Take distress to God first
   Before you speak, pray. Not a performance prayer. A surrender prayer. If you cannot pray honestly, you are not ready to speak honestly.

6. Build tolerance for discomfort
   Practice being disappointed without becoming dangerous. Sit with no. Sit with tension. Let time exist without trying to force resolution through pressure. That is maturity.

◆

Closing Mirror

Manipulation gets outcomes and loses trust. Honesty protects trust even when outcomes are delayed. Manipulation feels powerful in the moment. Honesty builds authority over time. If you want a clean home, clean relationships, and clean faith, you cannot keep using dirty tactics.

◆

Chapter 3

Deception and Image Management

Core Lie

"If people see the full truth, I will lose respect, control, or security."
"So I will shape perception instead of submitting to reality."

Deception is not always a bold lie. Most of the time it is editing. It is leaving out the detail that would change the story. It is shifting emphasis depending on the audience. It is letting someone defend you based on a false version of events because it benefits you. Deception is protection of an image. Truth is exposure of a heart.

◆

How This Shows Up in Real Life

Deception shows up wherever you feel unsafe being fully known.

Selective storytelling

You tell the story in a way that makes you sound reasonable and the other person sound extreme. You omit what you said first. You omit how you reacted. You omit your tone. You omit your part.

You call it "context."

But the context is only included when it favors you.

Shifting narratives

You change your description depending on who is listening. One story for your friends. One story for church. One story for family. One story for your husband. And you tell yourself it is just "explaining it differently," but the truth is you are managing what each person concludes.

Half truth protection

You do not technically lie. You just let a misunderstanding stand. Someone assumes you were innocent. You stay quiet. Someone assumes you were mistreated. You stay quiet. Someone assumes you did not do it. You stay quiet. And silence becomes part of the lie.

Performance emotion

You present tears, outrage, shock, or confusion to sell innocence. Not because you are confused, but because confusion makes you look clean. You act hurt so you do not have to answer questions. You act surprised so you do not have to admit intent.

Spiritual deception

You hide behind religious language to block scrutiny. You use verses as cover instead of correction. You say "I forgive you" while still rewriting the story to avoid accountability. You say "God knows my heart" when your actions clearly reveal it. Deception is not just about facts. It is about motive. It is wanting the benefit of righteousness without the cost of righteousness.

◆

Biblical Pattern

Scripture has no respect for deception, even when it is subtle. Potiphar's wife stages a cry, tells a crafted story, and ruins an innocent man to protect her image. Genesis 39:14 to 18. Her sin was not only lust. It was image protection through false witness. Ananias and Sapphira present an offering as if it is total while secretly keeping back part. Acts 5:2, 8 to 9. They wanted the appearance of sacrifice without the reality. This is important. They did give. They just lied about what they gave. God treated that as lying to the Holy Spirit. Because God weighs truth, not performance. Jezebel writes letters in Ahab's name, hires false witnesses, and kills Naboth. 1 Kings 21:8 to 10. Deception becomes murder when it is allowed to grow. Deception always escalates because you have to keep protecting the first lie.

◆

False Version vs Godly Version

False version: "I am private"

Privacy is guarding what is not owed. Deception is hiding what is owed. Privacy is: I do not share every detail of my life. Deception is: I share enough detail to steer conclusions while hiding my accountability.

False version: "I am just venting"

Venting that poisons someone's reputation is not venting. It is narrative control.

Godly version: Truthfulness and clean speech

Truthfulness is refusing to edit reality to stay safe. It is telling the truth even when it costs you sympathy. Truthfulness is not oversharing. It is alignment. One story. One mouth. One reality.

Mirror Questions

- Do I leave out details that would change how the story sounds?
- Do I tell different versions of the same situation depending on the audience?
- Do I let misunderstandings stand when they benefit me?
- Do I use emotion to sell innocence?
- Do I get anxious when people compare stories?
- Do I feel threatened by direct questions?
- Do I exaggerate to sound more justified?
- Do I frame myself as the victim more than the participant?
- Do I hide behind "that's not what I meant" instead of owning impact?
- Do I use spiritual language to avoid accountability?

◆

Trajectory If Untreated

In marriage
Trust collapses because your partner cannot tell what is real. He starts verifying. He starts guarding. He starts recording details mentally because he expects shifting narratives. That is not intimacy. That is survival.

In friendships and church
You may gain allies short term, but you lose credibility over time. Eventually people notice the patterns. They notice the missing facts. They notice that every story ends with you clean and someone else dirty.

In faith

Deception hardens the heart because repentance requires truth. If you cannot tell the truth, you cannot repent. And if you cannot repent, you will keep performing spirituality while rotting internally. Deception produces outward polish and inward decay.

◆

Counter Trait: Truthfulness and Integrity

Core Truth

If the truth costs me something, it reveals what I was depending on. Truthfulness is not about looking good. It is about being clean. Truthfulness is when you stop protecting an image and start protecting alignment.

◆

How This Shows Up in Real Life

You say the part that makes you look bad. Early. Without being forced. You stop curating stories. You stop framing yourself as the reasonable one by default. You stop using timing and emphasis to steer what people conclude. You correct misunderstandings even when they benefit you. When someone defends you based on a false version, you interrupt it. "No, that is not accurate. I did do that." That single sentence will expose whether you love truth or love protection. Truthfulness is costly. That is why it is rare.

◆

Biblical Pattern

Nathan confronted David, and David did not rewrite the story. "You are the man." 2 Samuel 12:7. David could have defended, minimized, or punished the messenger. Instead, he said: "I have sinned against the Lord." 2 Samuel 12:13. No spinning. No image management.

No "but she."

No "you don't understand."

Just ownership. That is truthfulness. Not perfection. Ownership.

Replacement Practices

1. Practice first truth
   Say the key fact first, even when it weakens your case. Not after you are cornered. First.

2. One story rule
   Tell the same story the same way to everyone involved. If you feel the urge to change the details depending on the audience, that is deception trying to protect you.

3. Correct yourself in real time
   When you exaggerate or shade the truth, stop and correct it immediately. "That's not accurate. Let me say it properly." This breaks the habit of narrative control.

4. No ally recruiting
   Stop telling stories to people who cannot resolve the issue. Address the person involved directly. If you need counsel, ask for counsel without poisoning perception.

5. Confess motive, not just facts
   Do not only say what happened. Say why you did it. "I wanted to look innocent." "I wanted sympathy." "I

wanted control." "I wanted to avoid consequences." That is where repentance actually lives.

6. Accept the cost of truth
Truth may cost you being admired. Truth may cost you being defended. Truth may cost you being seen as the victim. Pay it. Because the alternative cost is your integrity.

◆

Closing Mirror

Deception keeps you safe short term and destroys you long term. Truthfulness exposes you short term and stabilizes you long term. A woman who tells the truth does not need to remember which version she told. She rests. When you stop protecting an image, you finally have room to be known.

◆

Chapter 4

Sexual Immorality and Sexual Leverage

Core Lie

If it feels good, it is permissible.

"If I can control desire, I can control the relationship."

"My body is mine to use however I need to secure affection, attention, status, comfort, or power."

Sexual sin rarely starts with a bed. It starts with an agreement in the heart. An agreement that says holiness is negotiable, and boundaries are only for people with less options. Sexual leverage is not just sleeping around. It is using sexuality as a steering tool, even inside a relationship. It is treating desire like currency.

◆

How This Shows Up in Real Life

This trait shows up in two main lanes. Open immorality, and strategic sexuality.

Open immorality

You entertain intimacy outside covenant and call it "connection." You keep private conversations that clearly cross lines. You keep emotional attachments that you hide. You meet up "as friends" but dress and behave like it is a date. You say you are waiting on God while still feeding desire in hidden places. You rationalize it because you are lonely. You rationalize it because you are hurt. You rationalize it because everyone does it. But Scripture does not call it normal. It calls it sin.

Strategic sexuality

You use sexual attention to gain leverage. You initiate affection after conflict to smooth consequences without addressing truth. You withhold affection to punish and pressure. You flirt to keep someone in orbit as a backup plan. You enjoy being desired more than being trusted. You post, dress, and position yourself to harvest eyes, then call it confidence. You let men buy access with money, favors, attention, or opportunity. It does not have to be explicit to be real. You know what you are trading. Sex becomes a tool for safety. And the moment sex becomes a tool, it stops being clean.

Deception that protects it

You hide your conduct, your intentions, or your history to preserve options. You downplay what happened. You rename it. You claim confusion when you were calculated. You call conviction "shame," so you can keep doing it.

◆

Biblical Pattern

Scripture shows sexual immorality as a door that opens other destruction, not just pleasure with consequences. Potiphar's wife does not simply desire Joseph. She pursues, pressures, seizes, then lies when refused. Genesis 39:7 to 18. Sexual sin joins manipulation and false witness fast. Proverbs 7 does not portray the seductress as spontaneous. She is calculated. She uses bold touch, smooth speech, religious cover, and timing. Proverbs 7:10 to 23. This is sex as a trap, not sex as intimacy. Numbers 25 shows sexual sin pulling Israel into idolatry. Women draw men into whoredom and sacrifices, and judgment falls. Numbers 25:1 to 3, 6 to 9. Sex becomes recruitment into rebellion. Revelation 2:20 names leadership that normalizes sexual immorality as a corrupting force in the church. Not because God is prudish, but because sexual sin trains the soul to ignore boundaries. Sexual immorality is never isolated. It always spreads. It always invites more compromise than you planned.

◆

False Version vs Godly Version

False version: "I am free."

False freedom says, my body, my choice. But it never stays free. It becomes ruled by appetite, attention, or fear of losing someone. False freedom always ends up in bondage, because desire is a terrible master.

False version: "I just have needs."

Needs do not authorize sin. Pain does not rewrite God's commands. Godly version: Sexual integrity and covenant intimacy Sexual integrity says: my body is accountable. Covenant intimacy says: my body is a gift under authority, not a bargaining chip. Integrity governs desire. Covenant makes desire safe.

◆

Mirror Questions

- Do I entertain attention that does not belong to my covenant?
- Do I flirt to stay desired even when I am not available?
- Do I use sex or affection to get peace without telling truth?
- Do I withhold closeness to punish or pressure?
- Do I keep emotional backups?
- Do I hide conversations, messages, or intentions?
- Do I dress or post to harvest attention and call it confidence?
- Do I rationalize sin because I am lonely or hurt?
- Do I delay boundaries until things escalate?
- Do I confuse desire with permission?

◆

Trajectory If Untreated

In marriage

Trust erodes because desire becomes unpredictable. A man cannot rest if affection feels strategic. A woman cannot rest if she is always managing attention and options. Conflict becomes dangerous because sex becomes a weapon or a reward. Intimacy becomes currency, not connection.

In character

Your yes and no lose weight. Boundaries become flexible. Conviction becomes muted. You start living double minded. Public purity language, private compromise.

In faith

Sexual sin trains your heart to resist authority. Because you cannot keep sin and keep reverence at the same time. You will either repent, or you will reinterpret Scripture to protect your behavior. That is the fork.

◆

Counter Trait: Sexual Integrity and Covenant Intimacy

Core Truth

My body is not autonomous. It is stewardship. Desire is not evil, but desire must be governed. Integrity says no early so it does not have to say no late. Covenant intimacy is not transactional. It is faithful, clean, and consistent.

◆

How This Shows Up in Real Life

Sexual integrity shows up before the moment. It shows up in what you do not entertain. What conversations you shut down early. What attention you do not feed. What private channels you do not open. Covenant intimacy shows up in clean motives. You do not give affection to avoid consequences. You do not withdraw affection to regain power. You do not use sex to keep someone attached while you stay unsubmitted. You guard access. You guard your mind. You guard your private life. You stop enjoying what you would not want exposed.

◆

Biblical Pattern

Joseph did not negotiate with temptation. He fled. "How then can I do this great wickedness, and sin against God?" Genesis 39:9. Integrity moves away, not closer. Song of Solomon shows desire inside belonging, not manipulation. "I am my beloved's, and his desire is for me." Song of Solomon 7:10. That is mutuality, not leverage. Desire under covenant builds. Desire used as a tool destroys.

◆

Replacement Practices

1. Flee, do not manage
   Stop telling yourself you can be close to temptation and stay clean. Cut off access early. End private channels. End late night emotional intimacy. End secret friendships that feed desire.
2. Remove all backup plans
   No orbit men. No emotional cushions. No private

attention sources. Backups kill covenant, even before you touch anyone.

3. Confession replaces secrecy
   Bring sin into the light. Confess to God plainly, and to a trusted older woman who will not flatter you. Secrecy is where this trait breeds.

4. Hard boundaries, not vibes
   Set clear rules for communication and time. No one on one private hangouts that read like dates. No flirty joking. No suggestive pictures. No attention farming. If you have to keep explaining why it is not wrong, it is already wrong.

5. Replace attention seeking with service
   You cannot feed lust and feed holiness at the same time. Shift your energy into: Scripture prayer work service real community Starve what feeds the flesh.

6. Let conviction do its job
   Stop calling conviction shame. Conviction is mercy. It is God warning you before you destroy yourself. If you keep numbing conviction, you will eventually numb joy too.

◆

Closing Mirror

Sexual sin promises power, but it always collects a debt. Integrity costs you pleasure now, but it protects peace later. The question is not whether you can attract. The question is whether you can be trusted. Because in the end, desire is easy. Covenant is rare.

◆

Chapter 5

Contempt

Core Lie

People are beneath me.

"If I treat them as small, I stay safe and superior."
"If I honor them, I lose power."

Contempt is not just "being annoyed."

It is an internal decision to remove value from someone. Contempt does not correct. It punishes. It does not build. It erodes. It is scorn in the heart that eventually shows up in tone, timing, facial expressions, jokes, and public disrespect.

◆

How This Shows Up in Real Life

Contempt is rarely loud at first. It is usually subtle, then it grows.

Dismissive tone

You answer like you are doing them a favor. Short replies. Eye rolls. Sighs. Smirks. You respond to honest thoughts like they are stupid. You treat questions like interruptions.

Mockery as power

You use sarcasm to win. You joke at someone's weakness so everyone laughs and you feel above them. You correct by humiliation, not by clarity. You do not say "that hurt me." You say something sharp enough to make them feel small.

Public disrespect

You embarrass your husband, leaders, or friends in front of others. You correct in public because it gives you control. You act like you are "just being real," but you are really marking your territory.

Spiritual contempt

You roll your eyes at obedience that looks humble. You treat sincere worship like it is embarrassing. You judge holiness by your taste.

You call reverence "extra."

Contempt toward correction

When someone confronts you, you do not weigh it. You dismiss it. You treat correction like an insult. You treat accountability like control. Contempt is how a woman protects pride. If you remove value from the person speaking, you do not have to face the truth they said.

◆

Biblical Pattern

Scripture shows contempt as a heart posture that brings real consequences. Michal despised David when she saw him worshiping the Lord with humility. 2 Samuel 6:16, 20 to 23. Her contempt was not about sin. It was about dignity. She wanted image, not humility. The story does not treat her as refined. It treats her as wrong. And the record ends with her barrenness, a sign that contempt broke something deep. Jezebel shows contempt at the moment of judgment. She paints herself, positions herself, and mocks Jehu from the window. 2 Kings 9:30 to 31. Contempt can look confident for five minutes. Then God answers it. Contempt always follows the same pattern: A person refuses humility. They mock what is right. They elevate themselves. Then the house fractures.

◆

False Version vs Godly Version

False version: "I am just honest."

Honesty is truth without manipulation. Contempt is truth mixed with poison. Honesty clarifies. Contempt shames. Honesty can be firm and still respectful. Contempt makes respect feel impossible because it needs the other person to feel small.

False version: "They deserve it."

Contempt always feels justified. That is why it is dangerous. It does not wait for righteousness. It declares itself righteous.

Godly version: Honor and sober respect

Honor does not mean you approve of everything. Honor means you treat people as weighty, created by God, accountable to God, and not yours to crush. Honor can confront. But it confronts to restore what is right, not to humiliate. Honor does not need sarcasm. Honor does not need an audience. Honor does not need to win.

◆

Mirror Questions

- Do I roll my eyes when someone is speaking?
- Do I use sarcasm to win arguments?
- Do I mock my husband or leaders in front of others?
- Do I speak about people with disgust instead of concern?
- Do I treat sincere worship as embarrassing?
- Do I dismiss correction quickly instead of weighing it?
- Do people feel respected after talking to me, or do they feel small?
- Do I enjoy being the smartest person in the room?
- Do I punish people with tone instead of addressing the issue plainly?
- Do I use jokes to cover bitterness?

◆

Trajectory If Untreated

In marriage

Contempt turns a home into a courtroom. Every mistake becomes evidence. Every weakness becomes ammunition. A man stops feeling safe. He either withdraws or he retaliates. Then both people start living guarded. When contempt grows, affection feels fake because respect is gone. You cannot build intimacy on scorn.

In motherhood

Children learn that love is conditional on performance. They learn to hide mistakes instead of confessing them. They learn to manage you, not trust you.

In faith

Contempt is spiritual pride wearing a clean outfit. You can become knowledgeable while becoming unteachable. You can become correct while becoming cruel. And that combination produces hypocrisy. Contempt makes repentance impossible because repentance requires humility.

◆

Counter Trait: Honor

Core Truth

People have weight because God gave them weight. Honor is choosing to see value even when you see flaws. Honor does not deny problems. Honor refuses to treat people like problems. Honor is not a compliment. It is a posture.

◆

How Honor Shows Up in Real Life

Honor shows up in speech first. You choose words that correct without crushing. You address the behavior without insulting the person. You stop correcting in public. You stop using jokes to expose someone. You speak about your husband and your leaders in a way that protects their dignity even when you need accountability. Honor also shows up in how you receive correction. You do not rush to defend. You listen.

You ask, "Is there truth here?"
You let the Lord use a person without needing to make the person look stupid to stay comfortable. Honor is self control under truth.

◆

Biblical Pattern

Abigail honored David in a tense moment. She did not flatter him. She restrained him from bloodshed with wise words and humility. 1 Samuel 25:23 to 33. Honor here is not weakness. It is strength that prevents damage. She treated him like a man accountable to God, not a man she could provoke. And her honor protected her household. Honor has fruit. Contempt has fallout.

◆

Replacement Practices

1. Cut sarcasm at the root
    Sarcasm feels intelligent, but it trains contempt. For thirty days: no sarcastic correction. If you cannot speak without sarcasm, do not speak yet.

2. Move correction to private
   If you have a real concern, speak privately. Public correction is often just power.
3. Practice weighty speech
   Before you speak, ask: Will this build, clarify, and restore, or will it shame and dominate If it shames, it is contempt. Stop.
4. Bless specifically
   Every day, say one specific honorable thing about your husband, your children, or someone you are tempted to despise. Not flattery. Specific value. Honor grows where you practice it.
5. Receive correction without punishing the messenger
   When corrected, do not smirk. Do not deflect. Do not attack tone. Say: "Give me a moment. I am going to think about that." Then actually think.
6. Repent of contempt by name
   Do not call it attitude. Call it contempt. "Lord, I have despised people in my heart. Clean it." If you keep renaming sin, you keep it.

◆

Closing Mirror

Contempt removes value to feel powerful. Honor recognizes value to stay righteous. Contempt makes you feel above people. Honor keeps you under God. If you want a home that feels safe, you cannot keep feeding scorn. Honor is the only soil where trust grows.

◆

Chapter 6

Pride

Core Lie

"I am the standard."

"I know better."

"If I humble myself, I lose status."

"If I submit, I become small."

Pride is not confidence. Confidence is stable. Pride is defensive. Pride is the need to stay above correction. It is the need to win. It is the need to be seen as the wise one, the strong one, the mature one, the one who cannot be wrong. And because pride cannot tolerate exposure, it always produces blame, sarcasm, and hardness.

◆

How This Shows Up in Real Life

Pride is not always loud. Sometimes it is spiritual and polished.

Cannot receive no

You treat boundaries as insults. You treat disagreement as disrespect. You turn "no" into a debate, a lecture, or a punishment. You do not just want a decision. You want acknowledgement that you were right.

Deflection and blame

When confronted, you shift focus fast. You attack tone instead of facing content. You bring up old failures to avoid current accountability. You turn one correction into a trial about what everyone else did wrong. Pride does not repent quickly. It negotiates.

Image obsession

You care more about looking righteous than being righteous. You explain, justify, and perform. You post the right things, say the right things, appear submitted, but your inner government is still self rule.

Status based spirituality

You judge worship, modesty, obedience, and humility by what you consider dignified. You treat lowly obedience as embarrassing. You treat reverence as weak. You treat holiness as something to display, not something to submit to.

Cutting speech

Pride enjoys being sharper than people. You use sarcasm to feel above. You use harsh "truth" to display superiority. You correct people in a way that makes them feel stupid, then you call it leadership. Pride wants to be right more than it wants righteousness.

◆

Biblical Pattern

Scripture shows pride as self rule against God's order, and it always produces consequences. Michal despised David's humble worship because she measured him by royal image. 2 Samuel 6:16, 20 to 23. Her pride was not loud. It was refined contempt. And it was still judged. Isaiah speaks of the daughters of Zion being haughty, obsessed with display, and God strips what they trusted in. Isaiah 3:16 to 24. The pattern is clear: pride ties identity to image, then God breaks the illusion. Pride is also shown in the way Potiphar's wife reacts to refusal. She cannot accept limits, so she frames Joseph to protect herself. Genesis 39:10 to 14. Pride does not accept boundaries. It punishes the person who enforces them. Pride always has the same spine: I will not be lowered. Even if truth demands it.

◆

False Version vs Godly Version

False version: "I have standards"

Standards can be righteous. But pride uses standards as a throne. Real standards correct you too. Pride standards only correct other people. Real standards are paired with humility. Pride standards are paired with contempt.

False version: "I am just confident"

Confidence can admit wrong. Pride cannot. Confidence does not need to win. Pride needs the other person to lose.

Godly version: Humility and teachability

Humility is not thinking you are nothing. Humility is accepting you are not God. Teachability is being willing to be corrected without retaliation. Humility is not passivity. It is submission under truth.

◆

Mirror Questions

- Do I struggle to admit when I am wrong?
- When corrected, do I explain, defend, and redirect instead of repenting?
- Do I need the last word?
- Do I treat disagreement as disrespect?
- Do I judge others' worship or obedience by my taste?
- Do I use sarcasm to feel above people?
- Do I correct in ways that shame instead of restore?
- Do I think my intentions should excuse my impact?
- Do I feel anger when someone sets a boundary with me?
- Do I secretly believe I am more mature than most people?

◆

Trajectory If Untreated

In marriage
Pride turns marriage into a competition. You cannot submit because you believe submission makes you smaller. You cannot be corrected because you interpret it as control. You cannot apologize cleanly because it feels like losing. A proud wife can look strong while quietly starving the home of peace. Over time, he either stops leading or he stops trusting. And once trust dies, the house becomes performance.

In friendships and community
People stop confronting you because it costs too much. They either flatter you, avoid you, or secretly resent you. You become surrounded by silence, and you call it respect.

In faith
Pride is the trait that makes repentance rare. You can stay in church and still be unsubmitted. You can quote Scripture while refusing to bow to it. Pride produces a woman who is spiritually loud and inwardly unchanged.

◆

Counter Trait: Humility and Teachability

Core Truth
God resists the proud and gives grace to the humble. James 4:6. Humility is the doorway to grace. If you want grace, you have to be reachable. Teachability is not letting everyone critique you. It is letting truth land, even when it stings.

◆

How Humility Shows Up in Real Life

You can say "you are right" without dying inside. You can apologize without attaching explanations and conditions. You can receive correction without punishing the person who brought it. You can hear a hard truth and sit with it instead of rushing to defend. You stop needing to be perceived as above. You start caring more about alignment than image. Humility shows up in speed. Pride delays. Humility responds.

◆

Biblical Pattern

David received correction from Nathan and did not crush the messenger. 2 Samuel 12:7 to 13. He did not pivot to blame. He did not defend his intention. He admitted sin. That is humility. Not perfection. Ownership. Also watch Abigail. She approached David with humility and wisdom, and her posture turned away unnecessary bloodshed. 1 Samuel 25:23 to 33. Humility is not weakness. It is restraint under God.

◆

Replacement Practices

1. Practice fast ownership
   When you are wrong, say it quickly. "I was wrong." No speeches. No courtroom.
2. Remove defense language from apologies
   Stop saying: "I'm sorry you feel that way." "I'm sorry but you..." "I didn't mean it like that." Say: "I did that. It was wrong. Will you forgive me."
3. Invite correction from one trusted source
   Not the crowd. Not social media. One trusted older

woman who is not impressed by you. Let her tell you the truth. Then do not punish her for telling it.

4. Kill the last word habit
End conversations without winning. If you keep talking until the other person yields, that is pride trying to stay above.

5. Replace sarcasm with clarity
Sarcasm is pride's favorite weapon because it shames while pretending it is humor. Say what you mean plainly, or be quiet.

6. Practice hidden service
Do something useful that no one will praise. Pride feeds on being seen. Humility grows in unseen obedience.

◆

Closing Mirror

Pride protects an image and loses grace. Humility loses an image and gains grace. Pride makes you uncorrectable. Humility makes you safe to lead, safe to love, and safe to be loved. If you want God's help, stop fighting to stay above.

◆

Chapter 7

Dishonor and Rejection of Headship

Core Lie

> "If I honor his lead, I lose myself."
> "If I submit, I become unsafe."
> "If I do not keep veto power, I will be controlled."

Dishonor is not the same as disagreement. Dishonor is contempt toward rightful authority. Dishonor is the posture that says:

> "I will cooperate only when I agree."
> "I will align only when it benefits me."
> "I will respect you only when you perform how I want."

Dishonor does not always look like open rebellion. Sometimes it looks like polite sabotage.

◆

How This Shows Up in Real Life

Conditional cooperation
You say yes with your mouth, then resist with your behavior. You drag your feet. You delay.

You "forget."
You do the opposite quietly. You comply just enough to avoid direct conflict, but not enough to align. Your standing policy becomes: I will submit when I agree. That is not submission. That is negotiation.

Public undermining

You correct him in front of others. You joke about him. You use sarcasm to signal that you are above his judgment. You speak about him in ways that make other people lose respect for him. Then you wonder why he feels distant, guarded, or harsh. You have been teaching the room that he is not weighty.

Outsider rule

You rally outsiders to overrule him. You leak private details to friends, family, or church people, not for healing, but for leverage. You build a pressure network that forces him to comply or look like the villain. You call it counsel. But the fruit is control.

Unilateral moves

You make decisions without him, then call him controlling when he reacts. Money, calendar, parenting, church attendance, boundaries with family. You move first, then act surprised when he expects alignment.

Weaponized intimacy

You use sex, affection, silence, or access as a steering wheel. You reward obedience with warmth. You punish leadership with coldness. That is not covenant intimacy. That is conditioning.

Spiritual disrespect

You treat headship like a man made concept, not a God given order. You argue Scripture like a lawyer to keep independence. You obey only when you can keep full control.

◆

Biblical Pattern

Scripture gives clear pictures of dishonor in women, and the pattern is consistent. Michal despised David in her heart and mocked him for humble worship. 2 Samuel 6:16, 20 to 23. Her dishonor came out as public scorn. Vashti refused a royal command in public assembly. Esther 1:12. The story treats it as insubordination, and she was removed. Samson's wife pressed him with tears, extracted his secret, then betrayed him. Judges 14:15 to 20. Delilah sold Samson for silver, wore him down, then delivered him. Judges 16:4 to 20. Those are not just immoral actions. They are covenant betrayal and power seeking. Jezebel used her husband's authority from the shadows to execute her will, corrupt the system, and secure what she wanted. 1 Kings 21:7 to 14. That is the extreme version of dishonor: usurpation. Dishonor always has the same shape: I will not come under. I will not align. I will keep power.

◆

False Version vs Godly Version

False version: "I just have opinions"

Having counsel is not sin. Dishonor is when your counsel becomes rebellion if he does not choose your preference. Godly counsel says: Here is what I see, here is why, and here is my appeal. Dishonor says: If you do not do it my way, I will punish, undermine, or sabotage.

False version: "I am protecting myself"

Protection is not permission to overturn God's order. If he is commanding sin, that is a different category. But most dishonor is not about sin. It is about control.

Godly version: Respectful alignment under God

Godly alignment is counsel plus submission. It is not silence. It is not pretending. It is not losing your mind. It is bringing your perspective plainly, then aligning when a righteous decision is made, unless the decision requires sin. It is honoring your husband as head while still honoring God as the highest authority.

◆

Mirror Questions

- Do I cooperate only when I agree?
- Do I slow walk decisions to regain control?
- Do I correct him publicly?
- Do I joke about him in a way that reduces him?
- Do I leak private issues to outsiders for sympathy and leverage?
- Do I make unilateral decisions and call him controlling when he reacts?
- Do I punish with coldness, silence, or withdrawal after he leads?
- Do I treat headship like a threat instead of an order from God?
- Would my husband say he rests because my word holds?
- Do I obey quickly, or do I comply while resisting inside?

◆

Trajectory If Untreated

In marriage

Dishonor kills a man's desire to lead righteously. He learns that leadership costs him affection, peace, and dignity. So he either stops leading or he starts forcing. Both outcomes are destructive. The house becomes unstable because authority becomes contested. Children learn to disrespect him because you model it. Even if you never say it directly, your tone teaches them.

In community

You become a woman who cannot be covered. You have strong opinions, but no alignment. You want accountability, but only on your terms. Over time, leaders avoid you. Not because they fear a strong woman, but because they cannot trust your posture.

In faith

Dishonor toward headship trains dishonor toward God. Because submission is a muscle. If you refuse it in the visible order, you will eventually refuse it in the invisible one too.

◆

Counter Trait: Godly Alignment and Respectful Submission

Core Truth

Submission is not inferiority. Submission is order. A submitted woman is not mute. She is governed. She can speak clearly, appeal wisely, and still align without sabotage. Respect is not something he earns by perfection. It is something you offer because God commanded order. Ephesians 5:22 to 24, 33. Colossians 3:18. 1 Peter 3:1 to 6.

◆

How This Shows Up in Real Life

You give counsel once, plainly, without theatrics. You do not repeat it until he caves. You appeal, then you align. You protect his dignity in public. You keep hard talks private. You stop recruiting outsiders to pressure him. You stop leaking his weaknesses for sympathy. You speak about him like you want other people to respect him. Because that is what you are building. You stop using intimacy as a steering wheel. Affection is not a reward for compliance. It is a consistent expression of covenant. You become dependable. Your yes holds.

◆

Biblical Pattern

Sarah is presented as an example of respectful posture, not because she was perfect, but because her general posture was submission and trust. 1 Peter 3:5 to 6. Also watch Abigail. She spoke truth, appealed wisely, and honored David's authority without provoking him or humiliating him. 1 Samuel 25:23 to 33. She did not need domination to influence. Her wisdom carried weight because her posture was clean.

◆

Replacement Practices

1. Private honor rule
   No public correction. No public sarcasm. No shaming stories. If you have a concern, take it to him privately.
2. Counsel then align
   Give your perspective clearly, then stop. If he decides in a righteous direction, align without sabotage. If you need review, set a time to revisit, not a hidden resistance campaign.
3. End leverage tactics
   No silent treatment. No intimacy withdrawal to punish. No affection spikes to control outcomes. Speak directly. Ask directly.
4. Close the outside pressure channels
   Stop telling the story to people who cannot resolve it. If you need counsel, seek it without poisoning perception. Do not use allies as weapons.
5. Train your submission muscle daily
   Pick one clear instruction from Scripture and obey it quickly. Submission is easiest to God when it is practiced consistently, not occasionally.

6. If commanded to sin, handle it righteously
   Proper appeal. Proper counsel. Proper authority. Not contempt theater. Not public embarrassment. Not retaliation. Acts 5:29 is real, but most women do not use it for sin. They use it for control. Do not lie to yourself.

◆

Closing Mirror

Dishonor says: I will cooperate when it benefits me. Alignment says: I will honor God by honoring order. Dishonor fights for control and loses peace. Submission yields control to God and gains stability. If you want a home with rest, you cannot keep contesting authority while claiming you want covering.

◆

Chapter 8

Quarrelsome and Contentious

Core Lie

"If I do not keep pressing my point, I will be overlooked."

"If I do not fight for my way, I will lose."

Peace means I got played, so conflict becomes my proof that I matter. A contentious woman does not just have conflicts. She produces an atmosphere. Strife becomes normal. Tension becomes home language. The house learns to brace. This trait is not about having standards. It is about loving friction.

◆

How This Shows Up in Real Life

The drip

You do not address an issue once and resolve it. You revisit it. You restate it. You reframe it. You reopen it. You bring up small faults until everyone feels like nothing is ever enough. You correct constantly, but nothing changes because the goal is not correction. The goal is release. You discharge irritation through argument.

Public correction

You call people out in front of others, then claim it is honesty. You embarrass to gain control. You prefer an audience because it makes your point feel heavier.

Tone as a weapon

You raise intensity to win. You use sharpness to keep people on defense. You interrupt. You talk over. You escalate. You do not let the other person land. Then when they get quiet, you call them avoidant or immature. But they are not quiet because they cannot talk. They are quiet because they are tired.

Win or lose mindset

Every disagreement becomes a contest. You need the last word. You need the concession. You need them to admit you were right. You treat compromise like weakness. You treat peace like surrender.

Bringing up the past

You keep old arguments alive because they are useful ammunition. You never truly forgive. You just store the offense and re use it when you need leverage.

◆

Biblical Pattern

Scripture describes contention like erosion, not like passion. "A quarrelsome wife is like continual dripping." Proverbs 19:13. It does not say she is like a storm that comes and goes. It says she is like water that never stops. "Better to live on a corner of the housetop than with a contentious wife." Proverbs 21:9. "Better to live in a desert land than with a contentious and vexing woman." Proverbs 21:19. Those statements are not poetic exaggerations. They are diagnostic. A contentious woman makes the home unlivable, not because she has concerns, but because she makes conflict a lifestyle. The Bible does not frame this as strength. It frames it as misery that pushes people away.

False Version vs Godly Version

False version: "I am just passionate"

Passion can be righteous. But contention is not passion for truth. It is appetite for friction. Passion can listen. Contention cannot. Passion aims for understanding. Contention aims for domination. False version: "If I do not press it, nothing will change" This is the lie that justifies endless arguing. But constant pressure does not produce maturity. It produces withdrawal, deception, and resentment. Godly version: Peace making and wise speech Peace making is not silence. Peace making is skill. It is knowing how to speak truth without stirring wrath. It is knowing when to stop. It is knowing how to correct privately and briefly. It is choosing building over winning.

◆

Mirror Questions

- Do people relax when I enter a room or brace for conflict?
- Do I keep bringing up the same issue after it has been discussed?
- Do I need the last word?
- Do I correct in public to make my point stronger?
- Do I raise my tone or intensity when I am not getting agreement?
- Do I interrupt or talk over people?
- Do I reopen old arguments to win new ones?
- Do I confuse peace with losing?
- Do I feel satisfied only when the other person yields?

- Do I use conflict to discharge stress instead of taking my stress to God?

◆

Trajectory If Untreated

In marriage

Contention teaches a man that home is not rest. It is court. He starts staying busy, staying away, or staying numb. Not because he does not love you, but because he cannot breathe. If he is passive, you will despise him. If he is strong, you will call him harsh. But your contention helped train both outcomes.

In motherhood

Children learn conflict patterns early. They either become anxious peace keepers, or they become combative copies. Either way, you pass down disorder.

In faith

Contention hardens into pride because you start trusting your arguments more than you trust God. You become a woman who can quote truth while constantly violating love. And you call that maturity.

◆

Counter Trait: Peace making and Gentle Wisdom

Core Truth

A soft answer turns away wrath. Proverbs 15:1. Peace making is not weakness. It is strength under restraint. A peace maker does not avoid truth. She learns how to deliver truth without multiplying fire. Peace making is choosing the goal of building, not the dopamine of winning.

◆

How Peace making Shows Up in Real Life

You can address an issue without escalating. You can say one sentence and stop. You can let the other person think without chasing them down emotionally. You can end a conversation without "closing it out" through domination. You correct privately. You keep a calm voice. You refuse to argue in front of children. You choose timing that helps resolution instead of timing that helps revenge. You learn the difference between:

This needs a conversation

This needs prayer

This needs patience

This needs to be covered by love Peace making is discernment, not passivity.

◆

Biblical Pattern

Abigail stopped David from shedding blood by approaching with humility and wise words. 1 Samuel 25:23 to 33. She did not escalate. She did not insult. She did not corner him. She brought truth in a way that he could receive, and it preserved life. That is peace making.

◆

Replacement Practices

1. Lower your tone on purpose
   Make your volume and pace slower than your emotion wants. If you cannot speak softly, you are not ready to speak.
2. Shorten your sentences
   Contention feeds on long speeches. Say the point in one or two sentences, then stop. Let silence exist without chasing it.
3. Private correction rule
   No public correction. No public sarcasm. No public fights. If it matters, handle it privately. If it does not matter, drop it.
4. Decide what is actually worth a conversation
   Before you speak, ask: Is this sin Is this wisdom Is this preference Stop treating preference like law.
5. Set a time limit
   Hard talks do not need to become endurance competitions. If the conversation is not resolving, pause and pray. Pick a time to revisit. Do not keep grinding until someone breaks.
6. Replace argument with intercession
   When you feel the urge to fight, pray first. Not performative prayer. Real prayer that admits what is

happening in you. Contention is often unprocessed fear and pride pretending to be righteousness.

◆

Closing Mirror

Contention feels powerful but it makes the house tired. Peace making feels slower but it makes the house livable. You do not prove strength by winning arguments. You prove maturity by building peace without sacrificing truth.

◆

Chapter 9

Greed, Materialism, and Serving Mammon

Core Lie

Money will keep me safe. Comfort will keep me stable. Status will keep me respected.

> "If I secure the bag, I can relax and stop needing God."

Greed is not only wanting more. Greed is trusting money as savior. Materialism is not only buying things. Materialism is building identity and security on things. And mammon is not just currency. It is the spirit of money as a master. You can go to church and still serve mammon. You can pray and still bow to lifestyle. You can quote Scripture and still be ruled by what you can control and purchase.

◆

How This Shows Up in Real Life

Hiding and controlling money

You hide spending. You hide debt. You hide income. You keep secret accounts or secret habits. You call it wisdom, but it is control and fear. You want the benefits of partnership while keeping unilateral power.

Luxury as identity

You use brands, trips, and aesthetics to signal value. You feel embarrassed by simplicity. You feel threatened by people who live content. You spend to feel seen, then you call it self care.

Using people as providers

You choose friendships and relationships based on what they can do for you. You keep men in orbit because they are useful. You keep access relationships, not covenant relationships. You measure people by resources, not fruit.

Religion as cover

You give publicly to be admired. You post generosity so people see you as righteous. You use God language to justify expensive desires. You talk about favor while neglecting obedience.

Bending truth to protect money

You shade facts. You manipulate outcomes. You justify dishonesty if it protects lifestyle. Greed will always pressure truth. Because truth is sometimes costly.

◆

Biblical Pattern

Scripture shows greed and mammon as a rival master, not a neutral tool. Rachel steals Laban's household gods and hides them. Genesis 31:19, 34 to 35. It is not just theft. It is grasping for security and inheritance, then lying to keep it. Delilah takes silver, presses Samson daily, then delivers him. Judges 16:4 to 20. Money makes betrayal feel reasonable. Jezebel engineers Naboth's death to secure property her house wanted. 1 Kings 21. Greed escalates into injustice fast. Ananias and Sapphira keep back part of the price and present the rest as if it is all. Acts 5:2, 8 to 9. They wanted the reputation of sacrifice while still clutching money. Jesus makes it plain. No one can serve two masters. You cannot serve God and mammon. Matthew 6:24. Not you should not. You cannot. One will rule.

◆

False Version vs Godly Version

False version: "I am just ambitious"

Ambition can be righteous when it is aligned with obedience and service. But greed is ambition without restraint and without reverence. Greed demands outcomes. Greed justifies sin for speed. Righteous ambition is willing to wait and work clean. Greed wants the blessing without the obedience.

False version: "I have standards"

Standards are not sin. But when standards are about image, they become idolatry. If your peace depends on luxury, mammon is already your master. Godly version: Contentment and open handed stewardship Contentment is not laziness. It is freedom. It is being able to have much without worshiping it, and to have little without panicking. Stewardship uses money as a tool under God. Greed uses God as a tool to get money.

◆

Mirror Questions

- Do I hide spending, debt, or income to keep control?
- Do I feel anxious when money is tight and act unfaithful under pressure?
- Do I choose people based on what they can provide?
- Do I enjoy attention more than integrity when giving?
- Do I spend to feel valuable or safe?
- Do I bend truth to protect lifestyle?
- Do I resent boundaries on money?
- Do I feel entitled to luxury even when needs are not covered?
- Do I treat generosity like a performance?
- Do I trust money more than I trust God?

◆

Trajectory If Untreated

In marriage

Money becomes a throne issue. You will fight over control, not just numbers. You will hide, defend, accuse, and keep score. A man cannot rest when he suspects financial secrecy. A woman cannot rest when she worships lifestyle, because lifestyle always demands more. The house becomes anxious. Not because there is no money, but because there is no peace.

In friendships and community

People feel used. They feel like they are only valuable when they are useful. Over time, real relationships thin out and transactional relationships increase.

In faith

Mammon slowly replaces God as functional savior. You start obeying only when it does not threaten comfort. You start interpreting Scripture to protect desire.

You start calling greed "favor."

Serving mammon produces a religious person with no reverence.

◆

Counter Trait: Contentment and Faithful Stewardship

Core Truth

God is my provider, not money. Money is a tool, not a master. Contentment is not a feeling. It is a decision to trust God's care and live within obedience. Faithful stewardship means you handle money in the light, with truth, generosity, and restraint.

How This Shows Up in Real Life

You are transparent. No secret spending. No hidden debt. No private financial life that undermines covenant. You live below your means without shame. You stop performing wealth to feel valuable. You stop spending to quiet insecurity. You give quietly. Not to be seen. Not to be praised. Because your heart is free. You choose relationships based on character, not access. You can say no to luxury without feeling deprived. Because your peace is not built on lifestyle.

◆

Biblical Pattern

The widow who gave two small coins did not give from excess. She gave from poverty. Mark 12:41 to 44. Her trust exposed the emptiness of those who gave for appearance. Jesus praises the posture, not the amount. That is stewardship with reverence. Matthew 6 teaches the mind shift: Seek first the kingdom of God, and trust the Father for what you need. Matthew 6:25 to 34. Mammon says worry, grasp, secure. God says obey, seek, trust.

◆

Replacement Practices

1. Full financial truth
   Bring all money into the light. If you are married, no secret accounts, no hidden spending, no private debt. If you are single, stop hiding your money story from accountability. Greed thrives in secrecy.

2. Budget as obedience
   Make a spending plan and submit to it. If you cannot obey a budget, you are being ruled by appetite.
3. Practice quiet generosity
   Give in ways no one can applaud. If you cannot give without being seen, mammon still owns your reputation.
4. Remove access thinking
   Stop measuring people by what they can do for you. Ask: Would I still want this person in my life if they had nothing to offer me If the answer is no, you are building a network, not a community.
5. Fast from luxury signals
   Take a set period and stop image spending. No status purchases. No look at me upgrades. No social media flex habits. Use the money margin for generosity and family needs.
6. Pray through Matthew 6 daily
   Not as poetry. As reprogramming. When anxiety rises, treat it like worship misdirection. Bring it back under God.

◆

Closing Mirror

Greed says: I need more to feel safe. Contentment says: God is enough to obey. Greed makes you chase. Contentment makes you steady. If money is your master, you will never rest. If God is your master, money becomes small again.

◆

Chapter 10

Jealousy and Envy

Core Lie

God is withholding from me.

"If someone else has what I want, it means I am behind, forgotten, or less valued."

"So I must compete, compare, and resent until life feels fair."

Jealousy and envy are not the same thing, but they sit in the same house. Jealousy guards what you believe is yours by covenant. It can be righteous when it protects what God gave. Envy craves what belongs to someone else. It wants to take it or see them lose it. Envy never has a righteous form. Most women do not want to admit envy because it sounds ugly. So they rename it discernment. Or standards.

Or "I just see through people."
But the fruit tells the truth.

◆

How This Shows Up in Real Life

Comparison obsession

You keep mental score. Her looks. Her ring. Her husband. Her attention. Her fertility. Her money. Her platform. You track it like a silent competition. You can congratulate her with your mouth and still feel tight inside.

Bitter interpretation

You interpret other women's blessings as personal insults. If she gets engaged, you feel exposed. If she is pregnant, you feel behind. If she is admired, you feel erased. You call it "triggered," but the trigger is entitlement.

Rivalry in relationships

You punish your husband or the men around you for not giving you what you see others receiving. You demand quick fixes to quiet your insecurity. You pressure for outcomes that only God controls, then blame people for not delivering.

Undercutting behavior

You shade her name in conversation. You do not lie outright. You imply. You make little jokes. You act cool and detached so you can pretend you are not affected. You feel a strange satisfaction when she stumbles.

Status chasing

You buy, post, dress, and position yourself to compete. Not because you love beauty or excellence, but because you need proof that you are not losing. Envy always needs proof. Because it cannot rest in God's timing.

◆

Biblical Pattern

Scripture shows envy and jealous striving as destructive pressure that turns relationships into battlefields. Sarah blames Abram when Hagar conceives, then mistreats Hagar. Genesis 16:5 to 6. The pain is real. The response is sinful. Jealousy turns into harshness and scapegoating. Rachel envies Leah and says to Jacob, "Give me children, or else I die." Genesis 30:1. Envy makes demands that are irrational and cruel. It puts pressure on a person to produce what only God gives. Envy also shows up in community dynamics. It produces slander. It produces sabotage. It produces divided friendships. It produces a home atmosphere where someone else's joy feels like a threat. Envy does not stay private. It leaks.

False Version vs Godly Version

False version: "I just want what is right" Wanting good things is not sin. Envy is when you cannot rejoice for others. Envy is when you interpret their blessing as your loss. Envy is when you want their reduction to soothe your insecurity.

False version: "I am just motivated"

Motivation can be holy. But envy is motivation mixed with resentment. Holy motivation says, I will work and wait. Envy says, I will compete and resent. Godly version: Gratitude and trust in God's portion Gratitude is not pretending you have everything you want. Gratitude is acknowledging what God has already given you without contempt. Trust is accepting that God's timing is not your enemy. A grateful woman can celebrate someone else without collapsing inside. Because her identity is not tied to being ahead.

Mirror Questions

- Do I feel irritation when another woman receives what I want?
- Do I find myself comparing constantly?
- Do I pressure people to deliver what only God can give?
- Do I reduce other women with sarcasm, coolness, or subtle shade?
- Do I secretly enjoy when someone who shines stumbles?
- Do I chase status signals to quiet insecurity?
- Do I interpret someone else's blessing as God neglecting me?
- Do I struggle to celebrate without feeling pain?
- Do I turn my longing into entitlement?
- Do I make decisions from comparison rather than conviction?

◆

Trajectory If Untreated

In marriage

Envy makes you ungrateful. Nothing is enough because you are measuring your life against someone else's highlight reel or someone else's timeline. A husband feels like he is constantly failing a standard he did not agree to. You stop seeing his efforts because your eyes are fixed on what you do not have. Envy poisons intimacy because gratitude dies.

In friendships

You cannot keep sisters close when you secretly resent them. You will either compete or withdraw. Either way, real friendship becomes rare.

In faith

Envy leads to accusation against God. You start treating God like an unfair distributor. Then you stop obeying with joy. Then you start obeying only to force outcomes. That is not faith. That is bargaining.

◆

Counter Trait: Gratitude and Content Trust

Core Truth

God is not withholding to harm me. God is shaping me, timing me, and training me. Gratitude is the discipline that breaks entitlement. Trust is the discipline that breaks comparison. You do not heal envy by getting what you want. You heal envy by changing what you worship.

◆

How This Shows Up in Real Life

You can congratulate her without needing to mention yourself. You can celebrate a sister's engagement, pregnancy, growth, or success without twisting. You stop using social media as a measuring stick. You stop turning your longing into pressure campaigns. You stop speaking about other women in ways that reduce them. A grateful woman does not need someone else to shrink so she can breathe.

◆

Biblical Pattern

Hannah had deep pain, but she brought it to God instead of turning it into rivalry. 1 Samuel 1:10 to 18. She wept, prayed, and poured out her soul. She did not attack Peninnah. She did not pressure her husband to fix what he could not fix. She took her longing to the only One who could answer it. That posture is the opposite of envy. It is trust under pain.

◆

Replacement Practices

1. Name envy as envy
   Stop calling it discernment. Stop calling it standards. Stop calling it "I just see the truth." Say it plainly: I envy her. Then repent.
2. Daily gratitude discipline
   Write down three specific gifts God has already given you. Not vague. Specific. Gratitude starves entitlement because it forces you to see reality.
3. Bless the woman you envy
   Not in your head. In action. Send a sincere message. Serve her. Pray for her good. Your flesh will hate this. That is why it works.
4. Fast from comparison sources
   For a set time, remove the inputs that feed envy. Stop stalking. Stop scrolling. Stop measuring. Use that time for Scripture, prayer, and service.
5. Stop pressuring people for God's job
   If it is in God's hands, stop demanding it from humans. Ask. Appeal. Pray. Wait. Do not punish.
6. Practice rejoicing out loud
   Train your mouth. Say good things about other women

without adding shade. Your speech will reveal your heart, and your speech can retrain your heart.

◆

Closing Mirror

Envy says: if she wins, I lose. Gratitude says: God is not confused about me. Envy creates rivalry and bitterness. Gratitude creates steadiness and peace. If you cannot rejoice for others, you are not ready for your own blessing, because you will not know how to steward it without turning it into a throne.

Chapter 11

Rebellion

Core Lie

"I have the right to govern myself."

Authority is a threat. Obedience is optional when it costs me comfort.

"If I submit, I will lose control, and if I lose control, I will not be safe."

Rebellion is not independence. Rebellion is refusal of rightful authority. It is the inner posture that says:

"I will comply when it benefits me, and resist when it costs me."

Rebellion does not always look loud. Sometimes it looks like delay. Sometimes it looks like selective obedience. Sometimes it looks like spiritual language used to justify disobedience. But the fruit is always the same. You are ungoverned.

◆

How This Shows Up in Real Life

Selective obedience

You obey what you like and ignore what confronts you. You can quote Scripture about blessings, but you resist Scripture about submission, modesty, repentance, forgiveness, and self control. You love the parts of God that feel comforting. You resist the parts of God that feel corrective.

Delayed obedience

You do not say no. You say later. You wait until the pressure fades. You wait until the moment passes. You wait until obedience no longer costs you anything. Delayed obedience is disobedience with better manners.

Defensiveness under correction

When confronted, you do not examine yourself. You examine the messenger. You attack tone. You attack timing. You attack intent. Anything to avoid the truth landing. Rebellion always tries to disqualify the person speaking so you can stay unchanged.

Resistance disguised as wisdom

You frame disobedience as discernment. You say:

I am just protecting my peace

I am just setting boundaries

I am just not tolerating disrespect

I am just following my gut

But Scripture is not governed by your gut. A boundary can be righteous. But rebellion uses boundaries as a shield against accountability.

Spirit of contradiction

You feel a reflex need to oppose. Even when the instruction is reasonable. Even when the counsel is wise. Even when the request is small. Rebellion does not want to be led. It wants to remain the reference point.

◆

Biblical Pattern

Rebellion is treated in Scripture as a spiritual issue, not a personality quirk. Saul is the clearest pattern. He did not deny God outright. He edited obedience. He spared what God said to destroy, then framed it as worship. "To obey is better than sacrifice." 1 Samuel 15:22. God's response is direct: "Rebellion is as the sin of witchcraft, and stubbornness is as iniquity and idolatry." 1 Samuel 15:23. That verse matters because it shows the connection: Rebellion is not small. It is competing authority. Israel shows the same pattern over and over. They wanted God's protection without God's rule. They wanted deliverance without submission. They wanted provision without obedience. Rebellion always tries to keep benefits while rejecting government.

◆

False Version vs Godly Version

False version: "I am strong"

Strength is not refusal. Strength is obedience under pressure. Rebellion is not strength. It is pride refusing to bow.

False version: "I am protecting myself"

Protection can be wise. But rebellion uses protection as an excuse to stay uncorrectable. If no one can speak to you, you are not protected. You are hardened. Godly version: Submission and prompt obedience Submission is not being controlled by humans. Submission is being governed by God. Prompt obedience is the proof that you fear God more than you fear discomfort. Obedience is not about emotion. It is about authority.

◆

Mirror Questions

- Do I obey only the parts of Scripture that fit my preferences?
- Do I delay obedience until it costs less?
- When corrected, do I attack tone instead of examining myself?
- Do I label accountability as control?
- Do I feel a reflex need to oppose leadership?
- Do I keep arguing until I regain veto power?
- Do I spiritualize disobedience as discernment?
- Do I want God's benefits without God's boundaries?
- Do I resist repentance because it feels like losing?
- Do I treat submission as weakness?

◆

Trajectory If Untreated

In marriage

Rebellion makes covenant unstable. You will not align unless you agree. You will not support unless you are centered. You will not submit unless you can keep full control. This forces either passivity or conflict. Either way, the home loses order.

In friendships and church

You become hard to lead and hard to help. People stop investing because every attempt to guide you turns into an argument. You end up isolated, then call it discernment.

In faith

Rebellion is the gateway to deception. Once you decide you will not submit, you start reinterpreting Scripture to protect yourself. You stop fearing God and start fearing outcomes. A rebellious woman can look spiritual while living ungoverned.

◆

Counter Trait: Prompt Obedience and Humble Submission

Core Truth

If God has spoken, timing is not mine. Obedience is not a suggestion. It is the evidence of who you serve. Submission is choosing to come under God's rule even when your flesh hates it.

◆

How This Shows Up in Real Life

You obey quickly, not after you feel ready. You stop negotiating instructions. You stop waiting for perfect clarity. You stop waiting until the conviction fades. You receive correction without punishing the messenger. You can say:

You are right

I was wrong

I need to change

Without adding speeches to protect your pride. You submit your preferences to Scripture, not Scripture to your preferences.

Biblical Pattern

When Jonah rebelled, the Lord disciplined him until obedience happened. Jonah 1 to 3. The pattern is not cute. It is severe. God did not debate Jonah. God governed him. And when Jonah finally obeyed, clarity returned. Rebellion creates chaos. Obedience restores order.

Replacement Practices

1. Same day obedience
   When convicted, act that day. Apologize that day. Stop the behavior that day. Cut off the relationship that day. Make the hard decision that day. Delay is how rebellion survives.

2. Stop defending
   When confronted, do not explain first. Examine first. Ask: Is this true Where is my responsibility What do I need to repent for

3. Submit your language
   Remove phrases that signal negotiation with God: "I know the Bible says, but..." "I just feel like..." "God understands..." Replace with: "It is written." "I will obey."

4. Practice being led in small things
   Choose to follow wise counsel in low stakes areas to retrain your submission muscle. If you cannot be led in small things, you will not be led in big things.

5. Stop calling correction control
   If you keep labeling correction as abuse, you will stay uncorrectable. Discern actual abuse, yes. But do not lie to yourself. Most women call correction abuse

because they hate being confronted.
6. Fear God again
   Rebellion grows where the fear of God is absent. Read passages about God's authority and judgment until reverence returns.

◆

Closing Mirror

Rebellion feels like freedom until you realize you are being ruled by your flesh. Obedience feels like death until you realize it is the path to life. If you want stability, peace, and a clean conscience, you cannot keep negotiating with God. Submission is not the loss of self. It is the end of self rule.

◆

Chapter 12

Witchcraft, Sorcery, and Spiritual Syncretism

Core Lie

God is not enough for what I need. God is too slow. God is too quiet. God's ways are too restrictive.

> *"So I will use forbidden spiritual power to get clarity, comfort, control, protection, or results, while still claiming God."*

Witchcraft is not a Halloween costume. It is power seeking. Sorcery is not aesthetic. It is manipulation through spiritual means. Syncretism is mixing. It is trying to blend God with other spiritual systems so you can keep control and still feel spiritual. This trait is not primarily about objects. It is about allegiance.

◆

How This Shows Up in Real Life

"Harmless" practices you keep excusing

Astrology as guidance

Tarot as insight

Crystals as protection

Manifestation rituals as creation

Energy cleansing as freedom

Ancestor veneration as comfort

Moon rituals as alignment

You call it culture, wellness, or curiosity. But curiosity is not neutrality when God already spoke.

Spiritual control language

You start talking like you have access other people do not. You say things like:

My spirit does not agree

The universe is speaking

My ancestors told me

God showed me, but there is no Scripture and no accountability It becomes a way to end conversations and avoid being challenged.

Mixing Jesus with forbidden sources

Bible verses next to astrology content. Prayer plus rituals. Worship music plus divination playlists. You want Jesus for peace and other spirits for control. That is not maturity. That is double minded.

Seeking power instead of holiness

You want results more than repentance. You want to feel powerful more than you want to be clean. So you trade submission for shortcuts. Keeping objects and media that keep doors open You keep the decks. You keep the crystals. You keep the books. You keep the accounts you follow. You keep the content that normalizes it. You say you are not serious, but you will not destroy it. That tells the truth. You are still loyal.

◆

Biblical Pattern

Scripture is blunt because this is not a small sin. It is spiritual treason. God forbids divination, sorcery, enchantments, familiar spirits, and consulting the dead. Deuteronomy 18:10 to 12. He does not forbid it because it is fake. He forbids it because it is a rival altar. When Saul could not get direction from the Lord, he sought a medium. 1 Samuel 28:7 to 20. Notice the pattern. Fear plus impatience leads to forbidden power. Jezebel is directly connected to whoredoms and witchcraft in the record. 2 Kings 9:22. In her pattern, control and counterfeit spirituality travel together. In Acts, believers who practiced magic did not keep it as a hobby. They destroyed it. Acts 19:19. That is repentance, not rebranding. The Bible treats these practices as a spiritual doorway, not an innocent personality trait.

◆

False Version vs Godly Version

False version: "I am just spiritual"

Spiritual does not mean safe. The spiritual realm is not a playground. If the source is not God, it is not neutral. It is another master. False version: "I still believe in God" Belief that refuses obedience is not faith. Faith submits.

False version: "This is just intuition"

God can guide. But divination is not intuition. It is a system that claims spiritual knowledge apart from God's order. Godly version: Pure devotion to God and tested guidance Godly spirituality is simple:

Prayer

Scripture

repentance

obedience

counsel under accountability

patience for God's timing

It is not experimentation. It is allegiance.

◆

Mirror Questions

- Do I consult astrology, tarot, crystals, or spiritual rituals for guidance or comfort?
- Do I mix Bible language with occult practices?
- Do I keep objects or media that I know God forbids?
- Do I want spiritual power more than I want holiness?
- Do I seek answers apart from Scripture because I want speed?

- Do I use spiritual language to control people or end accountability?
- Do I defend these practices more than I defend obedience?
- Do I fear the future more than I fear God?
- Do I treat God like one option among many?
- Have I refused to destroy what I claim I renounced?

◆

Trajectory If Untreated

In your home

You bring confusion into the atmosphere. A mixed altar does not produce peace. It produces instability, fear, and disorder. Children learn that truth is flexible. They learn God is not Lord, He is a tool.

In relationships

You become harder to correct because you can always claim spiritual justification. Disagreement becomes "they do not get it spiritually."

Correction becomes "they are judging me."

That posture isolates you.

In faith

Syncretism slowly kills reverence. You start using God language while living in contradiction. Then conviction fades. Then repentance feels unnecessary. Then you build a religion that serves you. That is not faith. That is self worship with candles.

◆

Counter Trait: Exclusive Devotion and Spiritual Cleanliness

Core Truth

God does not share His throne. You cannot drink from the cup of the Lord and the cup of devils. 1 Corinthians 10:21. Spiritual cleanliness is not a vibe. It is separation. You cannot keep doors open and claim peace. Peace comes with alignment.

◆

How This Shows Up in Real Life

You stop seeking hidden knowledge. You stop chasing signs. You stop outsourcing your discernment to systems God hates. You accept that God's timing is part of His authority. You stop forcing clarity through forbidden means. You live with one altar. You become teachable again because your authority is Scripture, not your experiences or your feelings.

◆

Biblical Pattern

Acts 19 gives the model: destroy what is tied to bondage. Acts 19:19. Not donate. Not sell. Not store in a box. Destroy. Deuteronomy 7:25 to 26 warns not to bring an abomination into the home. The principle is simple. Do not house what God hates and expect blessing.

◆

Replacement Practices

1. Total removal
   Remove every object, book, deck, charm, crystal, altar item, and ritual tool. Do not sell it. Do not give it away. Destroy it. If it damages souls, you do not profit from it and you do not pass it on.

2. Confess the motive
   Say what you were really chasing: control comfort certainty identity protection revenge power Repentance starts when you tell the truth about desire.

3. Cut off inputs
   Unfollow accounts. Stop listening to teachers who normalize it. Stop consuming content that makes it feel cute. You cannot starve a sin while feeding it daily.

4. Replace the ritual with Scripture and prayer
   When anxiety rises, do not reach for a sign. Reach for the word. Read Scripture out loud. Pray plain prayers. Wait. The habit you build in fear reveals who you trust.

5. Submit guidance to testing
   If you believe God is guiding you, test it: Does it align with Scripture Does it produce humility Does it require obedience Does it withstand counsel If it bypasses Scripture and accountability, it is not God.

6. Clean the home
   This is not superstition. It is allegiance. Remove items. Stop the practices. Set the atmosphere with prayer, Scripture, and order.

◆

Closing Mirror

Witchcraft promises control and delivers bondage. Obedience costs you control and delivers peace. Syncretism feels flexible and ends in confusion. Exclusive devotion feels narrow and ends in stability. If you want a clean life, you need a clean altar.

◆

Chapter 13

Vindictiveness

Core Lie

> "If I do not make them pay, justice will not happen."
>
> "If I forgive, I am approving what they did."
>
> "If I let it go, I will look weak and they will get away with it."

Vindictiveness is not the same as having boundaries. Vindictiveness is punishment as a lifestyle. It is the inner vow that says:

> "I will not rest until they feel what I felt."

And once that vow is in you, you stop being a woman seeking righteousness and you become a woman seeking payment.

◆

How This Shows Up in Real Life

Vindictiveness can be loud, but it is usually strategic.

Score keeping and delayed payback

You do not resolve conflict, you store it. You smile today, but you remember. You wait for leverage. Then later, when you have the upper hand, you strike. You punish when it is safest for you, not when it is right.

Withholding as punishment

You withhold warmth, affection, respect, help, access, or cooperation to punish a person for not giving you what you wanted. You call it boundaries, but the goal is not protection. The goal is payment.

Reputation damage

You do not address the person involved. You damage how others see them. You tell the story in a way that makes them look dirty and you look clean. You leak private details. You recruit an audience. Then you call it venting. Vindictiveness loves an audience because shame feels like a stronger punishment than truth.

Sabotage

You do small things that create problems. You "forget" important things. You create inconvenience. You delay. You miscommunicate. You subtly block progress. Then you act innocent.

Righteous anger theater

You claim moral superiority, but the goal is still revenge. You do not want repentance. You want them crushed. Even if they apologize, you keep stabbing because apology does not satisfy vindictiveness. Payment does.

◆

Biblical Pattern

Vindictiveness is always presented as destructive and ungodly, even when the person feels justified. Herodias held a grudge against John and wanted him killed, and she kept pressing until she got her outcome. Mark 6:19 to 28. This is vindictiveness with a polished face. She does not move on. She hunts. The unforgiving servant is the same heart posture. He receives mercy, then refuses to release someone who owes him. Matthew 18:21 to 35. The point is not money. The point is the heart that demands payment. Scripture gives a direct command that exposes vindictiveness as rebellion against God's role. "Vengeance is mine." Romans 12:19. That is not a suggestion. That is a boundary God sets around Himself. Vindictiveness is the act of taking a role that belongs to God and calling it justice.

◆

False Version vs Godly Version

False version: "I just want justice"

Justice is righteous. Vindictiveness is personal repayment. Justice aims to restore what is right. Vindictiveness aims to satisfy pain. Justice can be pursued through proper authority. Vindictiveness bypasses authority and becomes punishment through the flesh. False version: "If I forgive, I am letting them off" Forgiveness is not excusing. Forgiveness is releasing your right to personally collect. Forgiveness does not cancel consequences. It cancels revenge. Godly version: Forgiveness and release of justice to God Forgiveness is obedience. It is not emotion first. It is the decision to stop feeding punishment in your heart and stop acting like you are the judge. You can forgive and still set boundaries. You can forgive and still require repentance for trust. You can forgive and still use lawful processes when needed. But you stop being the executioner.

◆

Mirror Questions

- Do I keep offenses stored for later use?
- Do I withhold warmth or cooperation to punish?
- Do I damage someone's reputation to make them pay?
- Do I enjoy the idea of them suffering?
- Do I keep bringing up old wrongs after an apology?
- Do I sabotage in small ways when I feel wronged?
- Do I feel disappointed when consequences do not hit them?
- Do I pretend I am over it while still plotting?

- Do I confuse forgiveness with approval?
- Do I refuse to release revenge to God?

Trajectory If Untreated

In marriage

Vindictiveness makes your home unsafe. Your husband learns that any failure will be paid for later. So he hides. He withdraws. He lies. He stops sharing. Intimacy dies because trust cannot live where punishment is stored. You may call it accountability, but it is fear based control.

In motherhood

Children learn that mistakes are dangerous. They become anxious and secretive, or they become vindictive copies. Either way, you train a home where grace is missing.

In faith

Vindictiveness blocks your own mercy. A woman who refuses to forgive becomes spiritually dry, harsh, and suspicious. She can quote Scripture, but she cannot reflect God's character. You cannot cling to revenge and walk in peace. It will not happen.

Counter Trait: Forgiveness and Releasing Justice to God

Core Truth

God sees. God judges. God repays righteously. My job is obedience, truth, and clean boundaries, not revenge. Forgiveness is not denial. Forgiveness is surrender. It is saying: I will not keep eating this poison. I will not become what hurt me.

◆

How Forgiveness Shows Up in Real Life

You stop collecting evidence to win later. You stop bringing up old offenses as weapons. You address issues directly, cleanly, and in the light. You stop recruiting an audience to shame someone. You can say:

What you did was wrong

Here is the boundary

Here is what trust would require

And I release the desire to punish you That is forgiveness with clarity, not forgiveness with delusion.

◆

Biblical Pattern

Joseph had power to punish his brothers. He did not use it for revenge. Genesis 45, Genesis 50:19 to 21. He acknowledged the evil. He did not pretend it was fine. But he released personal vengeance. David spared Saul when he had a clean chance to kill him. 1 Samuel 24, 1 Samuel 26. David refused to take vengeance into his own hands even though Saul was wrong. That is the pattern of righteousness: You do not become a killer because you were threatened. You remain under God.

◆

Replacement Practices

1. Confess the revenge desire
   Do not act spiritual. Tell the truth. Lord, I want them to pay. I want them to feel it. I want them humiliated. I want control. That confession is the beginning of freedom.

2. Stop punishment tactics immediately
   No silent treatment designed to hurt. No withholding designed to train them. No sarcasm designed to shame. No sabotage. If you need a boundary, state it plainly and keep it.

3. Separate forgiveness from trust
   Forgiveness is owed. Trust is earned. You can forgive someone and still not let them back into private access. You can forgive and still require repentance and time. This prevents fake forgiveness that keeps reopening wounds.

4. Bring matters into proper authority when needed
   If a situation requires church leadership, use it. If it requires lawful processes, use them. If it requires separation for safety, do it. That is not revenge. That is

order. But do not use authority as a weapon. Use it as a guardrail.

5. Bless and pray for the person
   This is the opposite of feeding bitterness. Pray for their repentance. Pray for their good under God. Pray for your heart to be cleaned. Your flesh will resist. That is the point.
6. Release the story
   Stop replaying it. Every replay is you drinking the offense again. You cannot heal while rehearsing injury. Replace rehearsing with prayer and Scripture.

◆

Closing Mirror

Vindictiveness says: I will be okay when they suffer. Forgiveness says: I will obey God even if they never apologize. Vindictiveness chains you to the offender. Forgiveness breaks the chain. If you keep demanding payment, you will keep living in bitterness. If you release it to God, you finally get your mind back.

◆

Chapter 14

Disobedience and Stubbornness

Core Lie

No one tells me what to do.

"If I yield, I lose."
"If I comply, I am being controlled."
"My way is safer than obedience."

Disobedience is not always loud rebellion. Sometimes it is quiet refusal. Stubbornness is not strength. Stubbornness is resistance to being governed. A stubborn woman can still appear polite, spiritual, and capable. But she is unteachable, uncorrectable, and hard to lead because her yes is never fully yes.

◆

How This Shows Up in Real Life

"I heard you" with no change

You acknowledge instruction, then do nothing. You nod. You agree verbally. You act like you received it. Then you keep the same behavior. This is disobedience with manners.

The slow walk

You delay until people stop expecting it. You take forever to follow through. You wait until the urgency is gone. You wait until the person is tired. Then you say you forgot or you were overwhelmed. But the pattern reveals motive. Delay is a way to keep veto power without open conflict.

Argument as avoidance

You turn every instruction into a debate. You ask questions that are not questions. They are resistance. You focus on exceptions, edge cases, and hypotheticals so you never have to obey the plain command. Stubbornness is often intellectual. It sounds thoughtful. But it produces no fruit.

Refusal to accept consequences

You want freedom without cost. You want to do what you want, then be comforted when it backfires. You act offended when natural consequences come. You claim people are harsh when they stop covering you.

Defiant identity

You treat obedience like personality death. You call yourself:

I am just strong

I am just independent

I am just not the type to be told But Scripture does not care about that identity. God is not negotiating with your temperament.

◆

Biblical Pattern

Scripture treats stubbornness as a serious heart issue, not a cute quirk. Saul's problem was not ignorance. It was partial obedience. 1 Samuel 15. He heard God, then edited God. He kept what he wanted and called it sacrifice. God called it rebellion and idolatry. 1 Samuel 15:22 to 23. Israel's pattern in the wilderness was constant. They saw miracles, then resisted instruction. They complained, resisted, and refused to trust. The result was delay, discipline, and death for many. Numbers 14. Stubbornness always produces the same fruit: You waste years. You repeat lessons. You lose opportunities. Not because God is cruel, but because God refuses to reward resistance.

◆

False Version vs Godly Version

False version: "I am just firm"

Firmness can be good when it is anchored in obedience. Stubbornness is firmness anchored in self will. Firmness submits to truth. Stubbornness submits to self. False version: "I need to understand first" Understanding is good. But stubbornness uses understanding as a delay tactic. God often calls you to obey what is clear while the rest remains unclear. Godly version: Teachability and faithful follow through A teachable woman is not weak. She is governed. She can receive instruction, apply it, and change without making it a courtroom. She is reliable because her yes has weight.

◆

Mirror Questions

- Do I acknowledge instructions but resist change?
- Do I delay follow through until people stop expecting it?
- Do I turn every request into a debate?
- Do I focus on exceptions to avoid simple obedience?
- Do I get offended by consequences?
- Do I treat correction like disrespect?
- Do I keep doing what I want then ask for sympathy?
- Do I interpret leadership as control?
- Do I want covering without accountability?
- Do I struggle to keep my word?

◆

Trajectory If Untreated

In marriage

Disobedience and stubbornness make partnership impossible. Your husband cannot trust your agreement because you may quietly resist later. So he either stops leading or he starts forcing. Either way, peace dies. Your word becomes light. And when your word becomes light, everything becomes unstable.

In parenting

Children learn that instruction is optional. They learn to negotiate, delay, and resist because that is what you model. Then you end up parenting a mirror of yourself.

In faith

Stubbornness blocks growth. You stay in the same cycles for years. Not because you do not know truth, but because you will not apply it. You become a woman with knowledge and no fruit.

Counter Trait: Teachability and Faithful Follow Through

Core Truth

Obedience is not a loss. It is alignment. A woman who can be led becomes safe, reliable, and strong. Teachability is humility in motion. Follow through is integrity in action.

◆

How This Shows Up in Real Life

You obey what is clear without delaying. You can receive instruction and say: Understood, I will do that. Then you do it. You stop debating everything. You ask sincere questions to clarify, not to resist. You accept consequences without playing victim. You become dependable. A teachable woman does not need to prove she is strong. Her strength shows up as restraint and obedience.

◆

Biblical Pattern

Ruth is the opposite of stubbornness. She receives counsel from Naomi and follows through with humility and precision. Ruth 3. She does not argue. She does not negotiate. She obeys. And that posture is part of what God uses to bring redemption and covering. Teachability does not make you small. It positions you to be blessed.

◆

Replacement Practices

1. One instruction per day
   Pick one clear instruction from Scripture and obey it the same day. Not later. Same day. This retrains the rebellion muscle.
2. Turn agreement into action quickly
   When you say yes, take a concrete step immediately. Send the message. Make the appointment. Write it down. Handle the task. Stubbornness thrives in vague intentions.
3. Stop debating clear commands
   If Scripture is plain, do not negotiate it. Obey first, then grow in understanding.
4. Keep your word training
   Start small. Make commitments you can keep and keep them. Your integrity is built through repetition.
5. Receive correction with one sentence
   When corrected, do not explain. Say: Thank you. I will think about that. Then actually do.
6. Practice submission in low stakes areas
   Choose to be led in small things to build capacity. If you cannot submit when it is easy, you will not submit when it is hard.

◆

Closing Mirror

Stubbornness feels like strength, but it produces wasted years. Teachability feels humbling, but it produces growth. A woman who cannot be led cannot be covered. A woman who can be led becomes safe to build with.

◆

Chapter 15

Weak Discernment (Easily Fooled)

Core Lie

If it feels right, it must be God. If someone sounds confident, they must be correct.

"If I like what I hear, it must be truth."

Weak discernment is not innocence. It is exposure. It is living open to every voice, every trend, every flattering teacher, every emotional impulse, with no testing and no filter. It is letting desire make decisions while calling it spirituality.

◆

How This Shows Up in Real Life

Charisma overrides truth

You get moved more by confidence than by fruit. A strong personality feels like authority, so you follow the energy. You assume that boldness equals wisdom. You assume that passion equals truth. You assume that popularity equals confirmation.

You believe stories without verification

You repeat things because they sound believable, not because they are proven. You share screenshots. You spread rumors. You forward warnings. You tell yourself you are helping, when you are really just passing along untested claims.

"Always learning" with no obedience

You consume teachings constantly but you never land. You are always in a new revelation, a new word, a new trend. But your actual character does not change. Your obedience does not deepen. Your relationships do not get cleaner. Information replaces repentance.

Oversharing that pretends to be transparency

You tell private things to too many people and call it honesty. You expose your home. You expose your husband. You expose your friends. Then you act surprised when trust dies.

Desire becomes your compass

When you want something, you stop testing. You ignore red flags because you like the feeling. You ignore patterns because you want the outcome. Weak discernment is not just being naive. It is being led by desires while pretending you are led by God.

◆

Biblical Pattern

Scripture warns that predatory voices slip into households and take captive weak women who are loaded down and led by many desires. 2 Timothy 3:6. That is not a compliment. It is a warning. The pattern is simple: When desire is loud and testing is absent, deception is easy.

◆

False Version vs Godly Version

False version: "I am open minded"

Open mindedness is not a virtue when it means you have no filter. False openness is moved by emotion and novelty. It is impressed by newness, not proven fruit.

False version: "I am just trusting"

Trust in God is obedience. Blind trust in people is carelessness.

Godly version: Tested wisdom and discernment

Godly discernment is not suspicion. It is testing. It is weighing fruit over charisma. It is choosing truth over feelings. It is moving slow when emotions are loud.

◆

Mirror Questions

- Do strong personalities move me more than clear Scripture?
- Do I share stories I did not verify?
- Do I keep learning without deciding and obeying?
- When I feel desire or fear, do I slow down and test, or do I follow it?
- Do I confuse excitement with confirmation?
- Do I overshare private matters and call it transparency?
- Do I ignore patterns because I want the outcome?
- Do I get pulled into trends easily?
- Do I trust people fast, then act shocked when it costs me?
- Do I test fruit, or do I just like the sound of the message?

◆

Trajectory If Untreated

In relationships
You keep getting played. You attract manipulators because they can feel your openness. They learn your triggers, your desires, your vulnerabilities, and they steer you. You keep calling it bad luck. It is not luck. It is lack of testing.

In the church
You become unstable. You bounce between teachings, groups, leaders, and convictions. You become easy to recruit and hard to mature.

In your character
You become double minded. You call things God one day and call them wrong the next. Your yes stops meaning yes because it changes with your emotions. Weak discernment does not just make you confused. It makes you unsafe to build with.

◆

Counter Trait: Godly Wisdom and Discernment

Core Truth

Truth does not fear testing. God does not require impulsiveness. Discernment is the discipline of slowing down, weighing fruit, and refusing to let desire lead.

◆

How This Shows Up in Real Life

You do not move on charisma. You move on fruit. You verify before you repeat. You ask questions before you commit. You watch patterns before you trust deeply. You stop oversharing. You stop exposing people to feel connected. You stop letting desire decide, then asking God to bless it. You become steady. Not easily impressed. Not easily swayed. Not easily recruited.

◆

Biblical Pattern

2 Timothy 3:6 is not only a warning about predators. It is also a mirror. It shows what they target. They target women led by desires. So the solution is not just avoiding predators. The solution is becoming the kind of woman who is harder to capture.

◆

Replacement Practices

1. The pause rule
   When you feel urgency, excitement, fear, or attraction, pause. Do not decide in that emotional wave. Make yourself wait long enough for truth to surface.
2. Verify before you speak
   If you did not confirm it, do not repeat it. If you cannot prove it, do not spread it. Stop being the delivery system for untested claims.
3. Fruit over flair
   Before you trust a voice, ask: Does this person show humility Do they submit to Scripture Do they produce repentance and order Do they show clean relationships and self control If the fruit is rotten, the

charisma is irrelevant.

4. Stop calling desire "discernment"
   Say it plainly: I want this I like this I am scared I am lonely Then test the decision anyway.

5. Tighten your circle
   Not everyone deserves access. Stop telling private things to people who cannot help resolve them. Discernment protects trust.

6. Obedience is the proof of learning
   Information is not growth. Obedience is growth. If you keep learning but you are not obeying, you are not being trained. You are being entertained.

◆

Closing Mirror

Weak discernment follows feelings and calls it faith. Godly discernment tests, waits, and obeys truth. If you refuse testing, you will keep getting captured. If you learn discernment, you become steady, and steadiness is protection.

◆

Chapter 16

Disloyalty and Opportunism

Core Lie

Loyalty is only for people who keep me comfortable.

"If staying faithful costs me, I am allowed to pivot."

Relationships are tools, not covenants. Disloyalty is not always cheating. Sometimes it is betrayal through speech. Sometimes it is abandoning people when they are inconvenient. Sometimes it is switching sides to stay safe and liked. Opportunism is loyalty sold for advantage. A disloyal woman can still look friendly, supportive, and spiritual. But when pressure rises, her allegiance moves.

◆

How This Shows Up in Real Life

Screenshot culture betrayal

You take private conversations and forward them. You send screenshots to group chats. You re tell private details for entertainment or alliance building. Then you act surprised when trust breaks. You say you were just venting. But venting that exposes someone is betrayal.

Side switching for safety

When conflict happens, you move to the side that benefits you most. You do not stand in truth. You stand in advantage. You agree with whoever is strongest in the room. You agree with whoever gives you the most attention. You agree with whoever can protect you from consequences.

Abandoning when it costs

When someone is weak, stressed, depressed, or unpopular, you back away. You love people when they are useful and easy. You disappear when their needs require sacrifice. This is not love. It is consumption.

Disloyal speech

You speak about your husband or your friends in ways that reduce them. You vent to people who do not have covenant with you. You tell stories that make them look dirty and you look clean. You entertain disrespect from others by staying silent or laughing. Silence can be betrayal when it is agreement by convenience.

Opportunistic dating and orbit behavior

You keep men around as options. You flirt enough to keep the door open. You use attention as a cushion. You call it harmless, but you are building backups. That is opportunism. It makes covenant impossible because your heart stays divided.

◆

Biblical Pattern

Scripture shows disloyalty as betrayal of trust and covenant, and it always carries consequences. Samson's wife pressed him and handed him over to her people. Judges 14:15 to 20. Delilah took money and delivered Samson to his enemies. Judges 16:4 to 20. The pattern is simple: pressure plus profit equals betrayal. Judas is the clearest male example. A close one sold a man for money. That is the spirit of opportunism. It values benefit over loyalty. Even in everyday wisdom, Scripture honors loyalty as rare and weighty. A faithful friend loves at all times. Proverbs 17:17. That means not only when it is easy. Disloyalty is not just a relationship issue. It is a character issue.

◆

False Version vs Godly Version

False version: "I am protecting myself"

Protection can be wise. But disloyalty is not protection. It is betrayal. If you want protection, set boundaries cleanly. Do not secretly sell people out to stay safe. False version: "I am just being honest" Honesty does not require exposing private matters to outsiders. Honesty speaks truth to the person involved, not gossip to spectators. Godly version: Faithfulness and protective loyalty Faithfulness is staying aligned when it costs. Protective loyalty means you do not expose people for entertainment or alliance. A loyal woman is a safe place. Her mouth does not leak. Her allegiance does not shift. Her yes holds.

◆

Mirror Questions

- Do I send screenshots or repeat private conversations?
- Do I switch sides when pressure rises?
- Do I disappear when someone becomes inconvenient?
- Do I speak about my husband in ways that reduce him?
- Do I entertain disrespect from others by staying silent?
- Do I keep backup options in relationships?
- Do I flirt to keep doors open?
- Do I share private matters with people who cannot resolve them?
- Do I value being liked more than being faithful?
- Would people call me safe, or unpredictable?

◆

Trajectory If Untreated

In marriage

Disloyalty destroys covering. A man cannot rest if he thinks your mouth is open in the wrong rooms. He cannot lead if he fears private weakness will become public entertainment. If you leak, he will guard. If he guards, intimacy dies.

In friendships and community

People stop trusting you. They may still enjoy you socially, but they will not give you real access. You become a surface level person with surface level relationships.

In faith

A disloyal heart struggles to covenant with God too. Because covenant requires loyalty when feelings shift. If you abandon people easily, you will also abandon conviction easily.

◆

Counter Trait: Faithfulness and Protective Loyalty

Core Truth

Loyalty is not a mood. It is a decision. Faithfulness means you do not trade people for comfort. Protective loyalty means you guard what is entrusted to you.

◆

How This Shows Up in Real Life

You keep private things private. You do not forward messages. You do not leak conversations. You do not share weaknesses with outsiders. You confront directly. If you have a problem, you speak to the person involved. Not to a crowd. You do not entertain disrespect. If someone speaks against your husband or your friend unjustly, you stop it. You do not laugh. You do not pile on. You do not stay silent. You do not keep backup plans. Your heart is single. Your yes holds.

◆

Biblical Pattern

Ruth is a picture of loyal faithfulness. "Where you go, I will go." Ruth 1:16 to 17. That is not emotional poetry. That is covenant posture. She stayed with Naomi when Naomi had nothing to offer. That is loyalty without advantage. That kind of loyalty is rare because it costs. But it produces fruit, protection, and honor.

◆

Replacement Practices

1. Close your mouth training
   For thirty days, do not tell private relationship issues to anyone who cannot help resolve them. No group chats. No vague posts. No hinting. If you need counsel, seek one mature person and speak cleanly, not theatrically.
2. Stop screenshotting
   If you have a habit of forwarding messages, stop immediately. If you need accountability, tell the person you need help, do not expose them behind their back.
3. Confront directly
   If you are hurt, speak to the person involved. If you cannot speak, pray first, then speak. Do not leak.
4. Cut off orbit behavior
   Stop keeping backup men. No flirtation. No private emotional connections. No "just friends" situations that would not survive daylight.
5. Practice loyal speech
   Speak about your husband and your friends in a way that protects dignity. That does not mean lying. It means speaking truth with covenant honor.

6. Stand when it costs
   When pressure rises, choose faithfulness. Do not switch sides to stay liked. Do not abandon people to stay safe. Do not trade loyalty for comfort. This is character.

   ◆

Closing Mirror

Opportunism says: loyalty is for when things are good. Faithfulness says: loyalty is proven when it costs. A disloyal woman is fun until it matters. A faithful woman is rare, and rare is what builds real covenant.

◆

Chapter 17
Selfishness and Self Centeredness

Core Lie

"My needs are the highest priority."
"If I do not put myself first, I will be neglected."

People exist to meet me, not to be served by me. Selfishness is not self care. Selfishness is worship of self. It is the posture that says: What I feel is the main reality. What I want is the main goal. What I need is the main demand. A selfish woman can still look loving when things go her way. Selfishness is revealed when sacrifice is required.

◆

How This Shows Up in Real Life

Relationship as consumption
You measure relationships by what you receive. If they give you attention, you stay warm. If they disappoint you, you punish or withdraw. You support people when it benefits your image or your comfort. You disappear when you are not getting what you want.

Entitlement in conflict
You do not ask. You demand. You treat your feelings like authority. You treat disagreement like disrespect. You believe you deserve special treatment because you are stressed, hurt, or tired. Stress is real. But stress does not make you righteous.

One way empathy

You want compassion but you do not give it. You want patience but you do not offer it. You want understanding but you do not listen. You want grace but you keep score. You call people selfish when they set boundaries, but you do not see your own extraction.

Self focus in the home

The house adjusts around your mood. Everyone learns to read you. Everyone learns to manage you. Peace becomes dependent on whether you are pleased. That is not leadership. That is emotional dictatorship.

Spiritual selfishness

You pursue God primarily for what you can get. You pray for outcomes, not for holiness. You read Scripture for comfort, not for correction. You worship when it feels good, not as obedience. You treat God like a supplier instead of Lord.

◆

Biblical Pattern

Scripture calls selfishness what it is. It does not dress it up. In the last days, people will be lovers of themselves. 2 Timothy 3:2. Self love is not presented as healing. It is presented as a marker of decay. James describes fights and quarrels as coming from desires that battle inside. James 4:1 to 3. The issue is not only the conflict. The issue is lust for what you want. Selfish desire produces disorder because it makes you treat people like obstacles. Even Jezebel's story contains selfishness at its core. Ahab wants Naboth's vineyard. Jezebel makes it happen. 1 Kings 21. It is desire elevated above righteousness. Selfishness always produces injustice when left unchecked.

False Version vs Godly Version

False version: "I am just setting boundaries" Boundaries can be righteous. But selfishness uses boundaries to avoid serving anyone. If your boundaries only protect your comfort and never protect obedience, you are not wise. You are self centered.

False version: "I have trauma"
Trauma is real. But trauma does not authorize self worship. Pain explains, but it does not excuse.

Godly version: Selflessness and service
Godly selflessness is not being a doormat. It is choosing to love through sacrifice. It is choosing to consider others, not only yourself. It is choosing obedience even when it costs comfort.

◆

Mirror Questions

- Do I treat my needs like the highest law?
- Do people adjust their behavior to manage my mood?
- Do I demand instead of ask?
- Do I expect grace but offer little?
- Do I withdraw when I am not getting attention?
- Do I support people only when it benefits me?
- Do I feel entitled to special treatment because I am stressed or hurt?
- Do I pursue God mainly for what I can get?
- Do I struggle to serve when no one notices?

* Do I feel offended when sacrifice is required?

◆

Trajectory If Untreated

In marriage

Selfishness turns marriage into a one sided system. A husband becomes a servant to your emotions, your preferences, and your timing. Over time, he either becomes resentful, passive, or harsh. Either way, intimacy dies because partnership becomes extraction. A selfish wife will call a man selfish the moment he stops feeding her.

In motherhood

Children become caretakers. They learn to manage you instead of being led by you. They become anxious because peace depends on your satisfaction.

In faith

Selfishness produces a consumer Christian. You attend for benefits. You serve only when it feels good. You stop obeying when obedience costs you. You become spiritually immature but convinced you deserve more.

◆

Counter Trait: Selflessness and Servant Heart

Core Truth

Love is not self seeking. 1 Corinthians 13:5. Jesus did not come to be served, but to serve. Mark 10:45. Selflessness is not erasing yourself. It is ruling yourself. It is choosing to love in ways that cost, without needing applause.

◆

How This Shows Up in Real Life

You ask instead of demand. You can be disappointed without becoming dangerous. You can serve without being seen. You can consider your husband's load, your children's needs, and the health of the home, not only your own comfort. You stop making everyone pay for your mood. You bring your distress to God first, then speak cleanly. A selfless woman is not empty. She is governed.

◆

Biblical Pattern

The Proverbs 31 woman is not self centered. She considers her household, works with wisdom, and serves with strength. Proverbs 31:15, 20, 26 to 27. She is not weak. She is productive and outward focused. Also look at Dorcas. She was full of good works and acts of charity. Acts 9:36. Her life produced benefit beyond herself. That is the opposite of self love worship.

◆

Replacement Practices

1. Daily unseen service
   Do one act of service each day that no one can applaud. Clean something. Prepare something. Encourage someone quietly. Give without being seen. This retrains motive.

2. Replace demands with requests
   Say: I would like I need Can we Stop saying: You never You always If you loved me Demand language is selfishness wearing righteousness.

3. Mood responsibility rule
   Your emotions are yours to steward. No punishing the house because you are tired. No making everyone pay because you are irritated. If you need rest, say it, take it, and remain honorable.

4. Practice listening first
   In conflict, ask questions before you argue. Selfishness talks to win. Love listens to understand.

5. Give your distress to God first
   Before you confront, pray. If you cannot pray honestly, you are not ready to talk honestly.

6. Fast from self focus inputs
   Reduce inputs that feed entitlement. Endless comparison content Endless validation content Endless "you deserve" messaging Replace it with Scripture, prayer, and real community.

◆

Closing Mirror

Selfishness says: love me first, then I will be good. Selflessness says: I will obey God and love rightly even when I feel unseen. Selfishness consumes people. Selflessness builds people. If you want a home that feels safe, you cannot keep making yourself the sun and everyone else the planets.

◆

Chapter 18
Gossip, Slander, and Loose Speech

Core Lie

"If I talk about it, I will feel better."
"If I share it, I will be understood."
"If I expose them, I will feel powerful and protected."

Gossip is not harmless conversation. Slander is not venting. Loose speech is not just "being real." Gossip is spreading information that is not yours to spread. Slander is speaking in a way that damages reputation, whether fully true, half true, or twisted. Loose speech is talking without restraint, without purpose, and without fear of God. Your mouth reveals your government.

◆

How This Shows Up in Real Life

"Prayer request" gossip

You share someone's private issue under spiritual cover. You say: Pray for her, because she is going through a lot Then you give details that were never yours to disclose. That is not intercession. That is gossip wearing church perfume.

Screenshot and group chat culture

You forward messages. You drop voice notes that expose private conflict. You share arguments like they are entertainment. You call it processing. But it is betrayal.

Character assassination through tone

You do not have to lie to slander. You can slander by framing. You tell true facts with a tone that makes them look evil. You omit your part. You exaggerate their part. You imply motives you cannot prove. Then you say you did not lie. But you still murdered their reputation. Talking to people who cannot solve it You do not go to the person involved. You go to people who can validate you. You go to people who will take your side. You go to spectators. This spreads division and leaves the actual issue unresolved.

Habitual criticism

You always have something to say about someone. You spot flaws fast. You talk about them fast. Your mouth is trained to pick at people. That is not discernment. That is corruption.

◆

Biblical Pattern

Scripture treats the tongue as a serious spiritual issue, not a minor flaw. "The tongue is a fire." James 3:6. That means it spreads. It consumes. It burns what you did not intend. "A talebearer reveals secrets, but he that is of a faithful spirit concealeth the matter." Proverbs 11:13. That is a clear contrast. Faithful spirit does not leak. "A whisperer separates chief friends." Proverbs 16:28. Gossip breaks close relationships. "A false witness" and "he that sows discord among brethren" are included in what the Lord hates. Proverbs 6:16 to 19. That is not light language. Loose speech is not only social damage. It is spiritual decay.

◆

False Version vs Godly Version

False version: "I am just venting"

Venting becomes sin when it spreads what should be covered, when it poisons perception, and when it recruits allies instead of seeking resolution. Venting that damages reputation is slander. False version: "I am just being honest" Honesty is speaking truth with clean purpose. Gossip is speaking truth with dirty purpose. If your goal is emotional release and social power, you are not being honest. You are being destructive. Godly version: Discreet speech and direct confrontation Godly speech is restrained. It is purposeful. It is clean. It confronts the person involved, not an audience. It covers what should be covered and exposes what must be exposed through proper authority, not through impulsive talking.

◆

Mirror Questions

- Do I share private information under the cover of prayer or concern?
- Do I forward screenshots and private conversations?
- Do I talk about people to those who cannot help solve the issue?
- Do I exaggerate or frame to sound more justified?
- Do I speak about my husband in ways that reduce him?
- Do I feel relief after exposing someone?
- Do I enjoy being the person who knows the details?
- Do I assume motives and speak them as facts?
- Do I talk more when I am emotional?
- Would people call me safe with secrets?

◆

Trajectory If Untreated

In marriage

Loose speech destroys trust fast. A husband will not be vulnerable to a woman who leaks. He will guard his heart, his plans, and his weaknesses. And once a man guards, intimacy dies.

In friendships

People will still laugh with you, but they will not trust you. You become entertainment, not refuge. And over time, you will notice people stop telling you things. They do not hate you. They just do not feel safe.

In faith

A loose tongue can make you spiritually unclean. You can worship and still be sowing discord. You can pray and still be destroying reputations. God does not separate mouth from holiness. Your mouth is part of your holiness.

◆

Counter Trait: Discretion, Faithful Speech, and Direct Resolution

Core Truth

A faithful spirit conceals a matter. Proverbs 11:13. Faithful speech protects what is entrusted. Direct resolution means you take issues to the person involved, or to proper authority when needed, not to spectators.

◆

How This Shows Up in Real Life

You stop talking for emotional release. You pray instead of spreading. You stop forwarding private messages. You stop telling stories that make you look clean and others look dirty. You become a woman who can hold weight. When someone tells you something, it stays with you. When someone confides in you, you do not leak it. When someone offends you, you address them, not a group chat. That is mature.

◆

Biblical Pattern

Jesus outlines a clean pathway for conflict. Go to your brother privately first. Matthew 18:15. Not publicly. Not indirectly. Privately. The point is restoration, not humiliation. Discretion supports restoration. Gossip destroys it.

◆

Replacement Practices

1. No spectators rule
   If a person cannot help resolve it, they do not need to hear it. Stop telling friends, family, and random church people your private conflicts.
2. End screenshot culture
   Do not forward private messages. If you need help, talk without exposing private texts and without recruiting a mob.
3. Speak to the person involved
   If you have a problem, address it directly. Not with sarcasm. Not with hints. Not with posts. Direct.

4. Stop framing
   Tell the truth with full context, including your part. If you cannot include your part, be quiet until you can.
5. Discipline your mouth when emotional
   Do not talk when you are heated. Pray first. Wait. Then speak with restraint. Most gossip starts as emotional discharge.
6. Replace talking with intercession
   When you feel the urge to expose, pray. Ask God to deal with it and to cleanse your motives.

◆

Closing Mirror

Gossip feels like connection but it produces distrust. Discretion feels quiet but it produces safety. A loose mouth can destroy years of trust in one weekend. A faithful spirit builds trust slowly and keeps it. If you want to be a safe woman, your mouth has to be governed.

◆

Chapter 19

Immodesty and Lack of Discretion

Core Lie

"My value comes from being desired."
"If I do not display myself, I will be ignored."

Attention is proof of worth, so I must keep it coming. Immodesty is not just clothing. It is presentation for appetite. Lack of discretion is not just oversharing. It is exposure without wisdom. This trait is not about fabric length alone. It is about motive, invitation, and the kind of attention you are cultivating.

◆

How This Shows Up in Real Life

Dressing to be chosen, not to be covered You do not ask, is this appropriate. You ask, will they look. You wear things that put sexual emphasis first, then you call any reaction "their problem." Yes, men should have self control. And yes, you are still accountable for what you present and what you are trying to produce. Immodesty is often disguised as confidence. But confidence does not need eyes to survive. Attention hunger does.

Social media thirst presentation

You post angles, poses, and captions designed to harvest desire. It is not accidental. You know what you are doing. You may not post nude. You may still be immodest. You use subtlety as plausible deniability. But motive is still motive.

Public intimacy and boundary erosion

You flirt openly while claiming you are friendly. You allow physical touch, private jokes, and suggestive energy that invites pursuit. Then you act shocked when men interpret it as invitation. This is not innocence. It is carelessness, or it is strategy.

Oversharing private life

You expose yourself and others with no filter. You share private conflict, sexual details, relationship problems, and home issues publicly or with too many people. You call it transparency. But it is often attention seeking, validation hunting, or emotional dumping. Discretion is a form of modesty too. A woman who cannot cover her own mouth cannot cover her house.

Competing with other women

You do not just want to look good. You want to win. You dress and post to outshine, provoke, or signal that you are more desirable than the next woman. That is not beauty. That is rivalry dressed as style.

◆

Biblical Pattern

Scripture addresses outward adornment because God addresses motive. "I will therefore that women adorn themselves in modest apparel, with shamefacedness and sobriety." 1 Timothy 2:9. That verse is not mainly about oppression. It is about order and reverence. "Whose adorning let it not be that outward adorning... but let it be the hidden man of the heart." 1 Peter 3:3 to 4. The focus is not anti beauty. The focus is identity. Proverbs gives a blunt picture of beauty without discretion. "As a jewel of gold in a swine's snout, so is a fair woman which is without discretion." Proverbs 11:22. That is not polite language. It is diagnostic. Beauty without discretion becomes a waste and a spectacle. The pattern is simple: When a woman lives for eyes, she becomes easily steered by appetite, attention, and insecurity.

◆

False Version vs Godly Version

False version: "It is just how I express myself" Expression is real. But your expression is not neutral. If your expression is designed to invite lust, you are not expressing personality. You are offering bait. False version: "Men should control themselves" Yes. And you are still accountable for your motives, your boundaries, and the signals you choose to send. Two truths can be true at the same time. Humans hate that. Godly version: Modesty, discretion, and reverence Modesty is choosing honor over appetite. Discretion is knowing what to cover, what to keep private, what to share, and with whom. Reverence is presenting yourself like you belong to God, not like you belong to the marketplace of attention.

◆

Mirror Questions

* Do I dress for attention more than for honor?
* Do I enjoy being stared at?
* Do I post pictures designed to harvest desire?
* Do I flirt and call it friendliness?
* Do I overshare private details for validation?
* Do I feel anxious when I am not being noticed?
* Do I compete with other women through sexuality?
* Do I like the power of being desired more than the peace of being clean?
* Do I invite attention from men I would not want leading me?
* Do I blur boundaries then blame others for crossing them?

◆

Trajectory If Untreated

In marriage

Immodesty and lack of discretion create instability. A husband cannot rest if his wife is constantly broadcasting herself for public appetite. Trust gets eroded because the posture looks like availability. Oversharing also damages covenant because private matters stop being private. A home cannot be safe when the mouth is open in the wrong places.

In relationships and church
Discretion loss makes you unsafe. People will enjoy you, but they will not trust you. Women will keep distance because they do not feel covered around you. Men will misinterpret access because you have trained them to.

In faith
Immodesty trains self worship. You start measuring your worth by attention. Then you start fearing aging, fearing being unseen, fearing losing power. A woman ruled by appetite and attention will struggle to walk in reverence.

◆

Counter Trait: Modesty and Discretion

Core Truth
My body is not currency. My life is not public property. My worth is established by God, not by attention. Modesty is not shame. Modesty is government. Discretion is not secrecy. Discretion is wisdom that protects covenant and protects reputation.

◆

How This Shows Up in Real Life

You dress in a way that honors your body without advertising it. You can be beautiful without being provocative. You can be attractive without being available. You stop posting for thirst. You stop feeding male attention as a source of worth. You tighten your boundaries. You do not entertain flirtation that invites pursuit. You do not allow private access that looks like a door. You become selective with your words. You stop telling private things to public people. You stop exposing your home for sympathy. A discreet woman can be trusted. That is rare. That is valuable.

◆

Biblical Pattern

Sarah is described with emphasis on meek and quiet spirit, not because she was invisible, but because her posture was governed. 1 Peter 3:4 to 6. The Proverbs 31 woman is clothed with strength and honor. Proverbs 31:25. Not clothed with attention. Not clothed with seduction. Strength and honor. That is the standard.

◆

Replacement Practices

1. Motive check before you leave the house
   Ask one question before you dress: Am I aiming for honor, or am I aiming for appetite If the answer is appetite, change.
2. Social media audit
   Remove any content that was posted to harvest desire. Then change your posting rules: No seductive angles No attention fishing captions No private availability

signals If you cannot post without craving eyes, take a break until your heart is governed.

3. Practice coverage
Choose what stays private. Marriage conflict stays private. Sexual history stays private. Family wounds stay private. Only share with trusted counsel, not spectators.

4. Boundary clarity with men
No playful flirting. No private emotional intimacy. No late night personal conversations. No attention harvesting. If you are single, keep your posture clean. If you are married, guard your covenant like it matters.

5. Train contentment with being unseen
Do something in public without trying to be noticed. No performance. No checking reactions. No fishing. If being unseen makes you anxious, that is the idol talking.

6. Replace attention seeking with service
Serve in ways that do not center your appearance. Your soul needs a stronger identity than desire.

◆

Closing Mirror

Immodesty says: notice me so I can feel valuable. Modesty says: I belong to God, so I will present myself with honor. Lack of discretion says: everyone gets access. Discretion says: access is earned and private matters are covered. If you want peace, you cannot keep feeding a system that needs eyes to survive.

◆

Chapter 20

Harshness

Core Lie

"If I am gentle, I will not be respected."
"If I soften my tone, people will ignore me."
"So I must use sharpness, intensity, and pressure to stay in control."

Harshness is not the same as being direct. Harshness is force in your words. It is correction without restraint. It is truth delivered like a weapon. It is using tone, volume, sarcasm, and intimidation to get compliance. Harshness is often pride that learned how to sound like strength.

◆

How This Shows Up in Real Life

Sharp tone as default

You speak like people are constantly failing you. Even when you are right, you sound contemptuous. Even when you are calm inside, you keep a cutting edge because you like the power it gives.

Escalation to win

When you are not getting agreement, you increase intensity. You raise your voice. You talk faster. You repeat yourself with more force. You crowd the conversation until the other person yields. This is not communication. It is pressure.

Correction that humiliates

You do not just address behavior. You attack the person. You use words that label and crush. You speak in ways that make people feel stupid for not seeing what you see. You call it truth. But it is pride mixed with anger.

Harshness toward weakness

You have little patience for people who are slow, struggling, confused, or learning. You do not coach. You criticize. You do not build. You scold.

Harshness disguised as standards

You justify it by saying you have high standards. But standards do not require cruelty. Harshness is often impatience with the fact that other people are not you.

◆

Biblical Pattern

Scripture is clear that harshness multiplies conflict. Proverbs 15:1 shows the pattern. A soft answer turns away wrath, but grievous words stir up anger. Harsh speech does not resolve tension. It feeds it. Sarah dealt harshly with Hagar, and Hagar fled. Genesis 16:6. Harshness drives people away, even when you feel justified. Nabal answered David with harshness and contempt, and it nearly brought bloodshed to his house until Abigail intervened. 1 Samuel 25:10 to 13, 23 to 33. Harshness creates unnecessary war. The pattern is consistent. Harshness turns problems into battles.

◆

False Version vs Godly Version

False version: "I am just blunt"
Bluntness can still be governed. Harshness is bluntness with anger and pride. Bluntness can build. Harshness bruises. False version: "People only respond to force" That is a control belief. It assumes the only way to move people is to pressure them.

Godly version: Gentleness with firmness
Gentleness is not weakness. Gentleness is strength under control. Gentleness can still be clear. Gentleness can still confront. But it refuses to dominate and humiliate.

◆

Mirror Questions

- Do people tense up when I speak?
- Do I raise intensity when I am not getting agreement?
- Do I use sarcasm to correct?
- Do I feel powerful when I am sharp?
- Do I lose patience quickly when someone is slow or weak?
- Do I correct in ways that shame instead of restore?
- Do I justify harshness by calling it standards?
- Do I talk at people instead of with them?
- Do I feel entitled to harshness because I am right?
- Do I calm down only after the other person submits?

◆

Trajectory If Untreated

In marriage
Harshness trains distance. A husband stops bringing issues to you because he expects pain, not help. He either withdraws or retaliates. Trust does not grow where words feel unsafe.

In motherhood
Children become anxious or rebellious. They learn to hide mistakes instead of confessing them. They learn to avoid you instead of being shaped by you.

In faith
Harshness creates hypocrisy. You can talk about holiness while violating love. You can be correct and still be unrighteous in posture. Harshness is often the fruit of pride, not the fruit of the Spirit.

◆

Counter Trait: Gentleness and Governed Speech

Core Truth
Gentleness is strength that refuses to harm. God does not need me to be harsh to be effective. Gentleness is a command, not a personality option. Philippians 4:5 calls for gentleness to be known. Proverbs 15:1 shows gentleness turns away wrath. If harshness is about control, gentleness is about trust.

◆

How This Shows Up in Real Life

You speak with restraint even when you are upset. You can correct without shaming. You can confront without humiliating. You can disagree without attacking. You stop using sarcasm as a blade. You stop raising your voice to win. You learn to pause before you speak. You let the Holy Spirit govern your mouth. Gentleness does not mean you never address issues. It means you address them cleanly.

◆

Biblical Pattern

Abigail approached David with humility and wise speech, and she turned away bloodshed. 1 Samuel 25:23 to 33. She was not weak. She was restrained, wise, and effective. Gentleness prevented destruction. That is what governed speech does. It keeps the house from burning down over pride.

◆

Replacement Practices

1. Tone audit
   Before you speak, ask: Is my tone trying to build, or trying to dominate If it is trying to dominate, stop.
2. Remove sarcasm from correction
   Sarcasm is harshness pretending to be humor. Say what you mean plainly, or be quiet until you can.
3. Pause when emotion rises
   When you feel intensity rising, pause and pray. Do not talk while heated. Harshness is often just emotional discharge.
4. Short sentences rule
   Harshness grows during long speeches. Say the point

in one or two sentences, then stop. Let the other person respond.

5. Private correction rule
   Correct privately whenever possible. Harshness loves an audience because it wants to win. Gentleness cares about restoration.
6. Repent of harshness by name
   Do not call it attitude. Call it harshness. Confess it, then replace it with restraint.

◆

Closing Mirror

Harshness can get compliance and still lose the heart. Gentleness protects truth and protects trust.

Chapter 21

Doubtful or Lacking Faith

Core Lie

God might not come through for me. God might not be good to me. God might not act unless I force outcomes.

"So I will worry, control, and self save, then call it wisdom."

Doubt is not the same as having questions. Questions can be honest. Doubt is a posture. Lacking faith is not about a moment of fear. It is living like God is unreliable. It shows up as worry, panic, manipulation, rushed decisions, and disobedience dressed up as practicality.

◆

How This Shows Up in Real Life

Anxiety as default

You live braced. You assume the worst. You rehearse disaster. You cannot rest until you can control every variable. And when you cannot control it, you spiral.

Rushing God

You do not wait. You force. You pressure people. You take shortcuts. You compromise. You make moves out of fear, then ask God to bless what fear built.

Double speech

You talk faith but live panic. Your words say trust. Your habits say grasp. You pray, then immediately scheme. You ask God, then refuse to wait for His timing.

Interpreting delay as abandonment

If the answer is not immediate, you conclude God is withholding. So you stop obeying with joy. You start obeying to bargain.

Faith that depends on feelings

If you feel strong, you believe. If you feel weak, you collapse. That is not faith. That is mood worship.

◆

Biblical Pattern

Israel saw deliverance, then panicked at opposition. They feared giants more than they feared God. Numbers 13 and 14. The result was rebellion, complaint, and wasted years. Peter stepped out of the boat, then looked at the wind and began to sink. Matthew 14:28 to 31. The shift was not the water. The shift was focus. James describes the doubter as double minded, unstable. James 1:6 to 8. Jesus directly confronts worry as a faith problem, not a personality trait. Matthew 6:25 to 34. The pattern is consistent. Fear multiplies when trust dies. And fear will always try to replace obedience with control.

◆

False Version vs Godly Version

False version: "I am just realistic"

Realism that deletes God is not realism. It is unbelief with a nicer label. False version: "I have been through a lot" Pain is real. But pain does not get to rewrite God's character.

Godly version: Faith and steady trust

Faith is not pretending outcomes. Faith is obeying God while outcomes are unknown. Faith is not hype. Faith is consistency under pressure.

◆

Mirror Questions

- Do I live in constant worry and call it being prepared?
- Do I rush decisions because I cannot tolerate uncertainty?
- Do I compromise to secure outcomes because I fear waiting?
- Do I pray and then immediately self save?
- Do I interpret delay as God refusing me?
- Do I trust God only when I feel emotionally strong?
- Do I punish people for not fixing what only God can fix?
- Do I keep needing signs and reassurance before I obey?
- Do I believe God is good only when life is easy?
- Do I talk faith but live panic?

◆

Trajectory If Untreated

In marriage

A faithless posture produces control. You pressure. You micromanage. You interpret everything as threat. Your husband becomes a tool for calming your anxiety instead of a partner in mission. You demand certainty from him that only God can provide.

In character

You become unstable. High hope one day. Collapse the next. You start and stop. You commit and retreat. Double mindedness makes your yes weak.

In faith

You drift into functional atheism. You still say God, but you live like you are alone. Then you become prayerless, joyless, and easily tempted, because fear has become your master.

◆

Counter Trait: Faith and Steadfast Trust

Core Truth

God is faithful even when I feel unstable. I do not need certainty to obey. I need reverence. Faith is not demanding control. Faith is submitting to God's command and timing.

◆

How This Shows Up in Real Life

You can wait without spiraling. You can obey before you feel ready. You stop forcing outcomes through pressure, manipulation, or compromise. You do what is right, then you trust God with results. You stop making fear based vows. You stop trying to secure your life through shortcuts.

◆

Biblical Pattern

Abraham is presented as a man who believed God. Romans 4:20 to 21. His faith was not performance. It was trust in God's ability. Hannah brought her distress to God instead of controlling people. 1 Samuel 1:10 to 18. Faith does not deny pain. Faith refuses to let pain become the driver.

◆

Replacement Practices

1. Obey what is clear
   Stop waiting for feelings. If Scripture is clear, obey it now. Faith grows through obedience, not through debate.
2. Replace worry loops with prayer and action
   When anxiety rises, do two things only. Pray. Do the next righteous step. Then stop. Worry is pretending you can control outcomes by rehearsing fear.
3. Remove compromise from your toolkit
   Faith does not need dirty tactics. If you have to lie, manipulate, seduce, or pressure to get it, you are building with fear.
4. Build endurance
   Choose one discipline and keep it daily. Prayer Scripture silence service Consistency trains steadiness.
5. Stop demanding certainty from humans
   People are not God. Stop making your husband, friends, or leaders responsible for calming your internal fear. Bring fear to God first.
6. Reframe delay
   Delay is not abandonment. Sometimes delay is

protection. Sometimes delay is training. Sometimes delay is timing. Faith learns to wait without accusing God.

◆

Closing Mirror

Doubt says: I must secure myself. Faith says: I will obey and trust God to provide. Doubt produces control and panic. Faith produces steadiness and peace. If you keep living like God is unreliable, you will keep acting like you are God.

◆

Chapter 22

Idolatry

Core Lie

"I need this to be okay."
"If I have this, I will be secure, whole, and at peace."
"If I lose this, I will fall apart."
"So I will cling, compromise, and disobey to keep it."

Idolatry is not only statues. Idolatry is dependence. It is when something created becomes your functional god. What you fear losing most. What you trust most. What you obey most. What you protect most. What you prioritize over God. Idolatry is not always obvious because it can be built on good things: marriage, children, ministry, money, attention, and comfort. Good things become idols when they become absolute.

◆

How This Shows Up in Real Life

Idolizing a relationship

You need a man to regulate you. His attention is your peace. His approval is your identity. His presence is your stability. So you compromise truth to keep him. You tolerate disrespect to avoid abandonment. You use sex, silence, control, or drama to keep connection. You call it love. But it is worship.

Idolizing children

Your child becomes your meaning. You cannot let them be uncomfortable. You cannot let them be corrected. You cannot let them face consequences. You protect them from discipline because their pain feels like your failure. This produces entitled children and exhausted mothers.

Idolizing image and attention

You worship being desired, praised, and admired. You craft presentation to stay validated. You feel panic when attention dips. You feel anger when someone else is celebrated. You feel restless when you are unseen. That is idolatry, not confidence.

Idolizing money and comfort

You treat security like salvation. You fear lack more than you fear sin. You compromise to keep lifestyle. You delay obedience because it might cost comfort.

Idolizing control

You trust your ability to manage outcomes more than God's authority. You cannot rest unless you control everything. You interpret surrender as danger. So you micromanage life, people, emotions, and timing. Control is often the idol that hides behind every other idol.

◆

Biblical Pattern

Scripture treats idolatry as spiritual adultery because it is covenant betrayal. Israel repeatedly returned to idols because idols promised control and visible reassurance. Exodus 32 shows them building a golden calf after deliverance. Idols always show up when fear and impatience are present. Rachel stole household gods, hiding them as security and inheritance. Genesis 31:19, 34 to 35. This is not only theft. It is attaching to an idol for safety. Jezebel is a picture of idolatry in practice because she established false worship, promoted false prophets, and opposed the Lord's authority. 1 Kings 18, 1 Kings 21. Idolatry is never isolated. It becomes a system. Jesus states the core principle: you cannot serve two masters. Matthew 6:24. Idolatry is divided allegiance.

◆

False Version vs Godly Version

False version: "I just care a lot" Care is not sin. Idolatry is when care becomes dependence, and dependence becomes obedience. If you disobey God to keep it, it is an idol. False version: "This is what motivates me" Motivation can be healthy. Idolatry is when motivation becomes worship. Godly version: God first devotion and ordered love Godly love is ordered. You can love a husband, children, work, beauty, and peace, but you cannot worship them. The difference is priority and obedience. When God is first, you can love things without being ruled by them.

◆

Mirror Questions

- What do I fear losing the most?
- What do I think I need in order to be okay?
- What do I protect even when it costs obedience?
- What makes me anxious when it is threatened?
- What do I compromise truth to keep?
- What do I obey more consistently than God?
- What do I constantly think about and plan around?
- If God told me to surrender it, would I obey or panic?
- Do I use people as saviors?
- Do I trust control more than I trust God?

◆

Trajectory If Untreated

In marriage

Idolatry creates bondage. If a man is your god, you will tolerate anything to keep him or you will destroy peace trying to control him. If comfort is your god, you will compromise truth to protect lifestyle. If control is your god, you will turn the home into a pressure system. Idols never stay private. They govern behavior.

In motherhood

Idolatry produces either overprotection or resentment. You either smother them because you need them, or you resent them for costing you what you worship.

In faith

Idolatry makes Scripture negotiable. You start twisting passages that confront your idol. You start avoiding teachings that threaten your idol. You start obeying only when it does not cost your idol. That is how a person stays religious while staying unsubmitted.

♦

Counter Trait: Exclusive Devotion and Ordered Love

Core Truth

God is God. Everything else is a gift. A gift becomes dangerous when you treat it like a savior. Ordered love means I love people and things in their proper place, under God, not above Him.

♦

How This Shows Up in Real Life

You can enjoy things without clinging. You can lose things without collapsing. You can love people without compromising obedience to keep them. You can receive blessings without worshiping them. You stop making humans responsible for what only God can provide. You stop expecting relationships to save you from your own inner emptiness.

♦

Biblical Pattern

Abraham was willing to surrender Isaac when God commanded. Genesis 22. Whether you agree with the test or not, the point of the narrative is clear: God exposes what sits on the throne. Abraham did not have to understand to obey. He feared God. That is the opposite of idolatry.

◆

Replacement Practices

1. Identify your main idol plainly
   Do not be poetic. Is it attention Is it a man Is it money Is it comfort Is it control Is it children Is it reputation Name it.
2. Repent of worship, not just behavior
   Say: I have needed this more than I needed God. I have feared losing this more than I feared sin. I have disobeyed to keep this. That is real repentance.
3. Practice surrender daily
   Do one act that breaks the idol's control. If it is attention, be unseen on purpose. If it is control, allow someone else to decide something. If it is comfort, do something hard without complaining. If it is money, give generously in secret. If it is a man, cut off the compromising access.
4. Remove idol feeding routines
   Stop feeding it. Stop the stalking. Stop the comparison. Stop the flirtation. Stop the luxury flex. Stop the comfort addiction. Idols starve when you stop offering sacrifices.
5. Put Scripture in the throne seat
   Obey Scripture even when you feel resistance. Your

feelings will reveal what you worship. Your obedience will re order your worship.

6. Rebuild trust in God's sufficiency
Idolatry grows where God feels distant. Return to prayer and Scripture not as performance, but as dependence.

◆

Closing Mirror

Idolatry says: this is my life. Devotion says: God is my life. Idols always demand sacrifice. God also demands surrender. The difference is the fruit. Idols take and leave you empty. God governs and makes you whole.

◆

Chapter 23

Unfaithful

Core Lie

Commitment is only valid while I feel fulfilled.

"If I am dissatisfied, I am entitled to escape."
"If I keep my options open, I stay safe."

Covenant is negotiable when it costs me. Unfaithfulness is not only physical cheating. Unfaithfulness is covenant betrayal in any form. It is when your heart, your loyalty, or your intimacy is given to someone or something outside your covenant, while you still want the safety and benefits of covenant. Unfaithfulness can be physical. It can be emotional. It can be secretive attention feeding. It can be staying married in name while living single in posture. The thread is the same. Divided allegiance.

◆

How This Shows Up in Real Life

Emotional affairs that you excuse

You create a private bond with someone who is not your husband. Private jokes. Daily texting. Late night conversations. Sharing heart details you do not share at home. Telling him about your marriage problems. You say it is harmless because nothing physical happened. But you are giving away intimacy that belongs in covenant. And you know it, because you hide it.

Attention farming while committed

You keep receiving romantic attention like you are available. You entertain DMs. You accept flirty compliments. You let men speak to you in ways you would not allow in front of your husband. You like the feeling of being wanted more than you value being faithful. Unfaithfulness is often protected by the phrase: I did not do anything. But you fed something.

Keeping backup plans

You keep men in orbit. Not because you plan to cheat today, but because you want insurance. You keep old flames warm. You keep options open. You keep access. A woman with backups is already unfaithful in posture. Covenant cannot be built while you keep escape hatches.

Secret life behavior

You delete messages. You hide calls. You rename contacts. You keep your phone guarded. The hiding is the proof. Faithfulness does not need hiding. Only betrayal does.

Retreating from covenant responsibilities

You may not cheat physically, but you abandon faithfulness through neglect. You stop building the marriage. You stop honoring. You stop respecting. You stop being present. You live as if you are single inside the marriage, then you call it self care. That is not faithfulness. That is quiet abandonment.

◆

Biblical Pattern

Scripture frames unfaithfulness as adultery and treachery. The command is direct. You shall not commit adultery. Exodus 20:14. Proverbs describes the adulteress as a woman who forsakes the guide of her youth and forgets the covenant of her God. Proverbs 2:16 to 17. Notice what it highlights. Covenant betrayal. Malachi speaks of treachery against the wife of your youth. Malachi 2:14 to 15. God treats covenant betrayal as treachery, not as a personal preference. Israel is repeatedly described as unfaithful to God, chasing other gods like adultery. This is not about romance. It is about loyalty. Jeremiah 3 is filled with that frame. God uses that language to show that unfaithfulness is not a small error. It is spiritual betrayal. The pattern is consistent. Unfaithfulness is a divided heart that refuses covenant loyalty.

◆

False Version vs Godly Version

False version: "I was not getting my needs met" Needs matter. But unmet needs do not authorize betrayal. Faithfulness is tested when you are dissatisfied, not when you are happy.

False version: "Nothing physical happened"

The goal is not to stop right before the edge. The goal is to keep covenant clean. If you are hiding, bonding, feeding, and entertaining, you are already outside the spirit of faithfulness. Godly version: Covenant loyalty and guarded intimacy Faithfulness means your intimacy stays in covenant. Your private world is protected. Your emotional bonding is disciplined. Your access with the opposite sex is governed. Faithfulness means your heart is not for sale.

◆

Mirror Questions

- Do I have private conversations I would not show my husband?
- Do I entertain flirty attention while committed?
- Do I keep backup men or old flames warm?
- Do I delete messages or hide communication?
- Do I tell another man what I should tell my husband?
- Do I dress or post to attract romantic attention while married?
- Do I feel entitled to external attention because I feel unseen at home?
- Do I keep my phone guarded like I have something to hide?
- Do I withdraw from building the marriage and live single inside it?
- Have I justified betrayal in my mind before acting it out?

◆

Trajectory If Untreated

In marriage

Unfaithfulness breaks trust even before physical cheating. Suspicion grows. Distance grows. Respect dies. A man who cannot trust your loyalty will stop giving you his heart. And when a man stops giving his heart, the home becomes transactional. Even if the marriage stays, it becomes empty.

In children and family legacy

Unfaithfulness teaches instability. Children learn that covenant is optional and loyalty is conditional. They learn to keep secrets. They learn to split households in their hearts.

In faith

Unfaithfulness hardens the conscience. You start rationalizing. Then you start hiding. Then you start lying to protect the double life. Eventually you either repent or you build a new moral system to protect the betrayal.

◆

Counter Trait: Faithfulness and Covenant Integrity

Core Truth

Faithfulness is not a feeling. It is allegiance. Covenant integrity means I protect my marriage before it is threatened, not after it is damaged. Faithfulness is built through boundaries, honesty, and intentional investment.

◆

How This Shows Up in Real Life

You refuse private intimacy with outsiders. No late night emotional bonding. No secret friendships. No private flirtation. You shut doors early. When a conversation crosses a line, you end it. When a man gives energy that does not belong, you cut it off. You live in the light. No hidden messages. No secret calls. No guarded phone. You invest at home. You speak to your husband instead of seeking connection elsewhere. You address needs directly. You build intimacy with truth and patience.

◆

Biblical Pattern

Joseph fled temptation. He did not negotiate it. Genesis 39:9 to 12. Faithfulness is not only resisting the act. It is refusing the environment. Ruth is faithful in posture. She does not live divided. Ruth 1:16 to 17. That is covenant language. That is loyalty. Faithfulness always has the same theme. A single heart.

◆

Replacement Practices

1. Cut off secret channels
    If you are hiding communication, stop today. Delete the contact if needed. End the private access. Do not keep the door cracked.
2. Restore transparency
    If you are married, your phone should not be a fortress. Transparency does not mean you have no privacy. It means you have no double life.

3. No opposite sex intimacy rule
   No private emotional bonding with men who are not your husband. If it must be discussed, keep it public, brief, and appropriate.
4. Replace attention hunger with identity in God
   If you crave male attention, tell the truth about it. That craving is not confidence. It is hunger. And hunger makes people do stupid things. Bring it to God and rebuild identity where it belongs.
5. Invest in covenant on purpose
   Schedule time. Have hard conversations. Build connection. Pray together if possible. Faithfulness is not only avoiding betrayal. It is building what makes betrayal less appealing.
6. Repent fully if you crossed lines
   Do not minimize. Confess what you did. Cut it off completely. Accept the consequences. Rebuild trust through consistent truth.

◆

Closing Mirror

Unfaithfulness says: I deserve an exit when I am dissatisfied. Faithfulness says: I will honor covenant even when it costs. A divided heart creates a divided home. A faithful heart creates a place of rest. If you want a marriage that lasts, your loyalty cannot be negotiable.

Thank You Page: Thank you for reading this book. Not everyone is willing to sit with truth long enough for it to do real work. Finishing this book signals more than curiosity. It signals intention, reflection, and a willingness to grow beyond surface level faith. This project was created with care and conviction. Its purpose was never to condemn, but to clarify. If these pages helped you see patterns more clearly, name things more honestly, or recognize areas where growth is still unfolding, then this book has served its purpose. Transformation does not end with a final page. It continues in the choices made quietly, consistently, and without performance. If you would like to support future projects that aim to teach biblical truth in thoughtful and creative ways, you are invited to visit:

www.disciplekid.com

We are currently developing a Bible based anime project designed to present Scripture accurately and compellingly for the next generation. Your support helps place truth in spaces where it is often missing. Thank you for your time. Thank you for your openness. Thank you for taking your walk with God seriously. Last but not least, thank you to our cover model whom I love dearly, one of my best friends please follow and support her @lady_silk4lifebaby

www.ingramcontent.com/pod-product-compliance
Lightning Source LLC
Chambersburg PA
CBHW071743150426
43191CB00010B/1668